Edmund Husserl's Theory of Meaning

PHAENOMENOLOGICA

COLLECTION FONDÉE PAR H. L. VAN BREDA ET PUBLIÉE SOUS
LE PATRONAGE DES CENTRES D'ARCHIVES-HUSSERL

14

J. N. MOHANTY

Edmund Husserl's Theory
of Meaning

J. N. MOHANTY

Edmund Husserl's Theory of Meaning

THIRD EDITION

MARTINUS NIJHOFF / THE HAGUE / 1976

PRINTED IN THE NETHERLANDS

FOREWORD

In this work I have tried to present Husserl's Philosophy of thinking and meaning in as clear a manner as I can. In doing this, I had in mind a two-fold purpose. I wanted on the one hand to disentangle what I have come to regard as the central line of thought from the vast mass of details of the *Logische Untersuchungen* and the *Formale und transzendentale Logik*. On the other hand, I tried to take into consideration the immense developments in logic and semantics that have taken place since Husserl's major logical studies were published. It is my belief that no one to day can look back upon the philosophers of the past except in the light of the admirable progress achieved and consolidated in the fields of logic and semantics in recent times. Fortunately enough, from this point of view Husserl fares remarkably well. He certainly anticipated many of those recent investigations. What is more, a true understanding and appraisal of his logical studies is not possible except in the light of the corresponding modern investigations. This last consideration may provide us with some explanation of the rather puzzling fact that orthodox Husserlian scholarship both within and outside Germany has not accorded to his logical studies the central importance that they, from all points of view, unmistakeably deserve.

The present study of Husserl's logical theory certainly suffers from one limitation, and this must be stated right here in order to avoid any misconception about my intentions. I have not sufficiently taken into consideration Husserl's conception of a transcendental logic, which certainly is the culmination of his thoughts in this field. No final appraisal of Husserl is possible unless this is taken into account. I have however voluntarily limited myself to a humble task for two reasons: in the first place, much has been written by other writers on this aspect of

Husserl's philosophy, so that I have preferred to confine myself
to a somewhat neglected aspect. Secondly, I thought it better
to reserve a study of Husserl's transcendental philosophy for
a future occasion, and at this stage can only express the hope
that in the years to come I may be able to place my researches
in that field before the reading public.

As will be evident to a careful reader, I am far from accept-
ing all of Husserl's ideas. My great admiration for him has not
blinded me to the many defects in the details of his analysis.
Often I have sought *to interpret*, and it is only natural that in such
a work as this, exposition and interpretation cannot be sharply
sundered from each other. In the course of my interpretation
and reformulation of Husserl I have arrived at two fundamental
principles: these may be called *The Principle of Phenomenological
Discontinuity* and *The Principle of Complementarity*. According
to the first, a truly phenomenological philosophy should recognise radical discontinuities amongst phenomena of different
types, and should not seek to fill in gaps arbitrarily. According
to the second, there are alternate modes of describing the same
phenomenon: of such modes three have seemed to me basic, –
the ontological, the formal or linguistic, and the phenomenological or noetic. A sound phenomenological philosophy should
recognise that these three are not rivals *but complementary*.
These principles, that have been merely suggested in the present
work, would, I hope, receive more detailed treatment in a larger
work on Husserl that I am at present working on.

My thanks are due to Professors Josef König (to whom this
work is dedicated, and whose lectures have greatly influenced
my philosophical thought), Hermann Wein (under whom I
studied the Hartmannian brand of phenomenology) and Kalidas
Bhattacharyya (who read portions of this work in manuscript and
gave me the benefit of valuable comments). I am also grateful to
Prof. Marvin Farber for kind words of encouragement and to
Prof. H. L. Van Breda and the members of the editorial Com-
mittee of the *Phaenomenologica* for kindly sponsoring the publication of this work. Lastly, I wish to put on record my gratitude
to the students of my post-graduate classes in Calcutta during

the years 1957–60 with whom I had discussed the problem of meaning in great details. Without their stimulating comments, the present work would not have taken the form it has.

Calcutta, 1st December 1962   J. N. M.

CONTENTS

ABBREVIATIONS

References are to the editions of Husserl's works which have been used in this work

L.U.,I: *Logische Untersuchungen*. I. Band. Vierte Auflage (Halle, 1928).

L.U.,II,1: *Logische Untersuchungen*. II. Band. 1. Teil. Vierte Auflage (Halle, 1928).

L.U.,II,2: *Logische Untersuchungen*. II. Band. 2. Teil. Dritte Auflage (Halle, 1922).

F.u.t.L.: *Formale und transzendentale Logik* (Halle, 1929).

E.u.U.: *Erfahrung und Urteil. Untersuchungen zur Genealogie der Logik* (Hamburg, 1948).

Ideen: *Ideen zu einer reinen Phänomenologie und phänomenologischen Philosophie*. Erstes Buch. *Husserliana*. Band III (The Hague, 1950).

Krisis: *Die Krisis der europäischen Wissenschaften und die transzendentale Phänomenologie. Husserliana*. Band VI (The Hague, 1954).

INTRODUCTION

(to the Third Edition)

I

Since the first edition of *Edmund Husserl's Theory of Meaning* appeared in 1964, Husserlian scholarship has made great strides forward. Several new volumes of the *Husserliana* have appeared, making available a major part of Husserl's posthumous writings.[1] Several important studies have appeared on Husserl's philosophy in general and on his philosophy of language, logic and meaning in particular.[2] With the publication, especially of the English translation of the *Krisis*, Husserlian phenomenology has been received, amongst English speaking students, with a new wave of enthusiasm by those who find in the concept of the life-world the guiding clue to a many-sided foundational research which, for them, is a more promising and welcome alternative to the earlier essentialistic and consciousness-oriented approaches.[3] At the

---

[1] *Zur Phänomenologie des inneren Zeitbewusstseins.* Ed. by R. Boehm (Husserliana, X), The Hague: Martinus Nijhoff, 1966; *Analysen zur Passiven Synthesis.* Ed. by M. Fleischer (Husser.iana, XI), The Hague: Martinus Nijhoff, 1966; *Philosophie der Arithmetik.* Ed. by L. Eley (Husserliana, XII), The Hague: Martinus Nijhoff, 1970; *Zur Phänomenologie der Intersubjektivität* Ed. by I. Kern (Husserliana, XIII, XIV, XV), The Hague: Martinus Nijhoff, 1973; *Ding und Raum.* Ed. by U. Claesges (Husserliana, XVI), The Hague: Martinus Nijhoff, *Formale und transzendentale Logik,* Ed. by (Husserliana, XVII), The Hague: Martinus Nijhoff, 1973. Even when some of these texts had been previously published, the present editions contain numerous unpublished supplementary texts.

[2] The most important is P. Ricoeur, *Husserl: An Analysis of his Phenomenology,* E. Tr. by Ed. G. Ballard and Lester E. Embree, Evanston: Northwestern University Press, 1967. Three other works may be mentioned here: Pivcevic, *Husserl and Phenomenology,* Londen: Hutchinson, 1970; J. Derrida, *Speech and Phenomena.* E. Tr. by D. Allison, Evanston: Northwestern University Press, 1973; R. Sokolowski, *Husserlian Meditations.* Northwestern University Press, 1974.

[3] The works of Alfred Schutz and the phenomenological sociologists point in this direction. In general, see – so far as the foundations of logic are concerned – the two papers by L. Eley; "Life world Constitution of Propositional Logic and Elementary

same time, with the publication of the English translation of the important logical writings of Husserl,[1] a better understanding of and a renewed interest, in the English-speaking world, in Husserl's philosophy of logic and theory of knowledge is in the offing.[2] My own Husserlian researches have led to *The Concept of Intentionality* and to several papers in which I have developed my Husserl interpretation both from historical and systematic points of view.[3] It is against this background that I have undertaken to

Predicate Logic" (in Tyminiecka (ed), *Analecta Husserliana*, Vol. II, 333–353 and "Afterword to Husserl, Experience and Judgment: Phenomenology and Philosophy of Language" (in Husserl, *Experience and Judgment*, E. Tr. by James S. Churchill and K. Ameriks. Evanston: Northwestern University Press, 1973).

For issues and tensions between the consciousness-oriented and life world oriented approaches, see L. Embree (ed), *Life-World and Consciousness. Essays for A. Gurwitsch*. Evanston: Northwestern University Press, 1972.

[1] These are: *Formal and Transcendental Logic*. E. Tr. by D. Cairns. The Hague: Martinus Nijhoff, 1969; *Logical Investigations*. E. Tr. by J. N. Findlay. London: Routledge Kegan Paul, 1970; *Experience and Judgment*. E. Tr. by James S. Churchill and K. Ameriks. Evanston: Northwestern University Press, 1973. Also pertinent are: "On the Concept of Number; Psychological Analysis" E. Tr. by Willard. *Philosophia Mathematica*, IX, 1972, 44–52; "A Reply to a Critic of My Refutation of Logical Psychologism". E. Tr. by D. Willard, *The Personalist*, LII, 1972, 5–13; ' Letter to Frege" E. Tr. by J. N. Mohanty, in "The Frege-Husserl Correspondence", *Southwestern Journal of Philosophy*, V, 1974, 83–95.

[2] An influential paper has been D. Føllesdal, "Husserl's Notion of Noema", *Journal of Philosophy*, 66, 1969, 680–687. Two important books which deal with Husserl's logic and epistemology are: E. Tugendhat, *Der Wahrheitsbegriff bei Husserl und Heidegger*. Berlin: De Gruyter Verlag, 1967; and R. Sokolowski, *Husserlian Meditations*. Some noteworth papers are: C. Downes, "On Husserl's Approach to Necessary Truth", *The Monist*, 87–106; J. E. Atwell, "Husserl on Signification and Object", *American Philosophical Quarterly*, 6, 1969, 312–317; D. Willard, "The Paradox of Logical Psychologism: Husserl's Way Out", *American Philosophical Quarterly*, 9, 1972, 94–100; R. C. Solomon, "Sense and Essence: Frege and Husserl", *International Philosophical Quarterly*, 10, 1970, 378–401; R. Sokolowski, "The Structure and Content of Husserl's Logical Investigations", *Inquiry*, 14, 1971, 318–347. Two pertinent criticisms of some of Husserlian theses – especially of the concepts of reference and truth in Husserl – are to be found in: E. Tugendhat, "Phänomenologie und Sprachanalyse" in: R. Bubner (ed), *Hermeneutik und Dialektik*, Bd. II Tübingen: J. C. B. Mohr, 1970, 3–23; and G. Patzig, "Kritische Bemerkungen zu Husserls Thesen über das Verhaltnis von Wahrheit und Evidenz", *Neue Hefte für Philosophie*, Heft 1, 1972. The unpublished Stanford dissertations of D. Smith (*Intentionality, Noemata, and Individuation*, 1971) and R. T. McIntyre (*Husserl and Referentiality: The Role of the Noema as an Intensional Entity*, 1970) are interesting attempts to interpret Husserlian semantics with the tools of modal logic.

[3] *The Concept of Intentionality*, St. Louis: Warren Green, 1972. "Life-World and A Priori in Husserl's later Thought", *Analecta Husserliana*, III, 1974: "On Husserl's Theory of Meaning", *The Southwestern Journal of Philosophy*, V, 1974; "Husserl and Frege: A New Look at their Relationship", *Research in Phenomenology*, IV, 1974; "Consciousness and Life-World", *Social Research*, 1975.

write this Introduction to the third edition of this book. This essay will, within its brief scope, indicate some of the ways in which the exposition of the book needs to be supplemented, it will also review some of the more significant criticisms levelled against Husserl's theory of meaning as also some noteworthy attempts at interpreting it.

II

First, as to Husserl's Fregean distinction between meaning and reference. There is a philosophico-historical commonplace, a belief widely shared by Husserl scholars as well as Frege scholars, to the effect: (a) that Husserl came to abandon his own psychologism of the *Philosophie der Arithmetik* as a consequence of Frege's devastating review of that book in 1894; and (b) that Husserl simply took over the Fregean distinction between sense and reference but used a different terminology to express the same. I myself shared this belief at the time I wrote this book, although it was never stated as such in it. My researches have now convinced me that neither of the two components of this belief is tenable.[1] I can here only state – seemingly dogmatically – what seems to me to be a nearly correct picture of the situation. First, Husserl's *central* thesis in the *Philosophie der Arithmetik* does not come under his own account of psychologism in the *Prolegomena* and a large part of that thesis does survive the *Prolegomena's* attack on psychologism.[2] Frege, it would then seem, did not really understand Husserl's concern in *Philosophie der Arithmetik* when he accuses him of psychologism. In the second place, if what is still lacking in that early work is the distinction between meaning, reference and subjective representations (this is part of Frege's charge in his 1894 review), Husserl arrived at this distinction already in his 1891 review of Schröder's *Algebra der Logik*, and so prior to, and independently of, Frege's 1892 paper "Sinn und

[1] For a preliminary but detailed presentation, see my "Husserl and Frege: A New Look at their Relationship".

[2] O. Becker had shown how and to what extent the *Philosophie der Arithmetik* was genuinely phenomenological. The best analysis of "psychologism" in Husserl is to be found in M. Sukale's unpublished Stanford dissertation *Four Studies in Phenomenology and Pragmatism* (1971). D. Willard has recently argued that Husserl's concept of number of the *Philosophie der Arithmetik* was not psychologistic (See his paper on Husserl's concept of number in *The Southwestern Journal of Philosophy*, V, 1974, Husserl Issue).

Bedeutung". The Frege-Husserl correspondence of the year 1891 also bear testimony to it.[1]

It is then not so much, as Beth complains,[2] the case of Husserl's failing to understand the full implications of Frege's criticism of his (earlier and alleged) psychologism as Frege's failure to understand what *Philosophie der Aritmetik* was striving towards, viz. a middle ground between the Platonism of meanings and psychologism.[3] The fundamental concept upon which this middle ground was to rest is the concept of *act*, and the concept of act is the concept of intentional experience. The difference then between Husserl's sense-reference distinction and Frege's is not merely terminological, but lies deeper: it derives from the fact that Frege did not have Husserl's full-blown concept of intentionality. This difference may be formulated thus: It is true that both Frege and Husserl asserted the objectivity of meanings, as contradistinguished from the subjectivity and privacy of mental states. For both, the thesis of the objectivity of meanings is incompatible with any thesis which makes them real components of mental states. But for Frege mental states are nothing but immanent and private episodes. Meanings may be *apprehended* by a mental act, but they are neither real constituents of the mind nor in any other sense related to it. For Husserl, mental states are intentional. Though founded on immanent, private data, an act, in so far as it is intentional, has ist correlative meaning which is yet objective. This peculiar, and for Husserl, decisive notion of intentional correlate gives him a concept of objectivity that is both weaker than, and less naively ontological than Frege's. The crucial point then is this: meanings, for Frege, are meanings of signs (words, sentences); for Husserl, they are meanings of expressive *acts* or speech acts.[4]

---

[1] E. Tr. by me in: *The Southwestern Journal of Philosophy*, V, 1974.

[2] E. W. Beth, *The Foundations of Mathematics*. Revised Edition. Harper Torch Books, 1964, p. 353.

[3] My exposition of Husserl's theory of meaning was made to rest on this strategy. One drawback of my use of this strategy was to give the readers the misleading impression as though Husserl himself was following it. The decisive influence in this regard was not Frege, but Lotze (as Husserl himself says in Logical Invesitgations, I, 218), a fact whose significance for philosophy of logic D. Willard has tried to work out in his "The Paradox of Logical Psychologism: Husserl's Way Out". One cannot also disregard the fact that in this regard Lotze was a major influence also on Frege.

[4] E. Tugendhat is thus right in saying that Husserl's theory of meaning begins with the intentional point of view, but wrong when he says that the results of the Fifth Investigation influence those of the First. The entire *Logical Investigations* in fact is

Meanings are 'ideal contents', 'intentional correlates' of acts, rather than self-subsistent entities. There is ample justification then for saying that while Frege's *Sinne* belong to his ontology, Husserl's meanings do not.[1]

Furthermore, as is well-known, Frege seems to have been led to his sense-reference distinction by his attempt to find reasons why the sentences 'a = a' and 'a = b' have different cognitive values so that whereas the former is analytic and a priori, the latter, if true, extends our knowledge and cannot always be a priori validated. This difference in cognitive value cannot be accounted for if we suppose either that the identities were between the things named by the signs 'a' and 'b' or that the sentences were about the signs themselves. In the former case, the two sentences 'a = a' and 'a = b' should have the same cognitive value, in case 'a = b' be true; in the latter case, the sentence 'a = b' could not express true knowledge, since our use of signs is arbitrary and we could designate the same things by some other signs or some other things by the same signs. Hence in order that 'a = b' could have the cognitive value it has, Frege concludes, there is "connected with a sign (name, combination of words, letter), besides that to which the sign refers, which may be called the reference of the sign, also what I should like to call the *sense* of the sign, wherein the mode of presentation is contained."[2]

It seems to me that Husserl never explicitly thematised this Fregean problem. The earliest context in which Husserl introduces the sense-*Vorstellung* distinction is provided by Schröder's account of equivocal and univocal names. Thus Husserl wrote: "... he (Schröder) lacks the true concept of the meaning of a name. That requirement of univocity is also expressed in the form: 'The name shall be of a ... constant meaning.' However, according to the relevant discussions ..., the author identifies the

meant to be a phenomenology of 'logical experiences' or acts. (Cp. Tugendhat, "Phänomenologie und Sprachenanalyse")

My exposition of Husserl's theory of meaning needs to be read in the context of Husserl's full-blown theory of intentionality; only then the account will be self-sustaining.

[1] The distinction between Husserlian essences and meanings is pertinent in this context. This distinction is more often overlooked than not. 'Essence', for Husserl, is an ontological concept, 'meaning' or 'noema' a phenomenological concept. Cp. *Ideen* III, 58.

[2] Frege, "On Sense and Reference", in: *Translation from the Philosophical Writings of Gottlob Frege*. Edited by P. Geach and M. Black. Oxford: Basil Blackwell, 1966, 56–78, esp. p. 57.

meaning of the name with the representation (*Vorstellung*) of the object named by the name, from which the striking consequence follows, to be sure, that all common names are equivocal."[1]

In the *Logical Investigations* the decisive text[2] occurs in a section in which Husserl refers to the same theme of equivocal names and contends that if meaning were the same as *Vorstellung*, all names would be equivocal proper names.[3] The sense-reference (*Bedeutung-Gegenstand*) distinction is introduced in the Schröder review in the context of the question, if an expression such as 'round-square' is meaningless (*unsinnige*) or not. Schröder, according to Husserl, confuses between two different questions: namely, whether there belongs to a name a *Sinn* and whether an object corresponding to it exists or not.[4] Increasingly, this second problem becomes more central to Husserl's thinking and corroborates his distinction between mere understanding and knowing (itself traceable to that between symbolic or inauthentic thinking and non-empty, authentic thinking of ch. XI of the *Philosophie der Arithmetik*). If meaning lay in intuition, purely symbolic thinking would be 'insolubly enigmatic';[5] if meaning were the same as the object, 'golden mountain' would be meaningless.[6]

Locating meaning in the expressive act is a move that brings Husserlian thinking about language close to some of the later Wittgensteinian analysts. For both, 'language' is founded on 'speech'; for both speech act is the primary phenomenon. But how is the 'speech act' to be understood? For the analysts, who cannot get rid of a deep suspicion of the usefulness of any concept of the inner, the concept of an act is the concept of a sort of rule-governed behavior. For Husserl, the speech act is an act in the sense of being an intentional experience, which has its sense and its reference. Speaking is a mode of consciousness. Husserl wants to return to this mode of consciousness, reflectively to the consciousness of speaking, to the living act of speaking rather than the observed act.

[1] Husserl's review of Schröder's *Algebra der Logik* in: *Göttingische gelehrte Anzeigen*, I, 1891, pp. 243–278, esp. p. 250.

[2] *Logical Investigations* (J. N. Findlay's English Translation), I, p. 287. (after this to be referred as LI).

[3] LI, I, p. 288.

[4] *Göttingische gelehrte Anzeigen*, I, 1891, p. 250.

[5] LI, I, p. 303.

[6] LI, I, p. 293.

III

Husserl, as is well known, reduces communicative speech to monologue, and actual speech to phantasised speech in order to exclude the function of intimation (or *Kundgabe*) from the essence of speech. I have contended in the text (pp. 15–16) that this Husserlian move is misleading in so far as it runs the risk of leading us back to psychologism and consequent relativism, and seems unnecessary for, and even incapable of, sustaining the thesis of the ideal objectivity of meanings. It is important however to recognise the true nature and motivation of this move.[1] It is undeniable that there is a certain harmony between this reduction and the general thesis of transcendental idealism, the reduction to pure consciousness, but it is as necessary to recognise this harmony as to clearly perceive where its limitations are. Looking back from the egology of the *Cartesian Meditations*, one does understand the need for location speech within the privacy of one's inner life; keeping in mind the role of phantasy in eidetic reduction (not yet, in the *Logical Investigations*, thematised as a method – though, to be sure, operative) in extracting the essence of a thing, one sees why, with a view to discovering the essence of speech act, Husserl should have turned from actual speech to phantasised speech. Again, in view of the thesis asserted in the *Ideas I* that meaning is the expression[2] one understands, that this identity requires that the outer, i.e. the sensible, aspect of an expression (the visual mark or the sound) shall be 'reduced', so that in phantasised inner speech the two aspects, the act of expressing and the act of meaning, become almost indistinguishable. Further, is not, according to Husserl, *Sprachlichkeit* an essential feature of consciousness[3] and not a mere contingent state? In that case, it has to be shown that even upon reduction to the purely

[1] J. Derrida seems to me to be wrong in contending that by excluding the intimating function through his reduction of speech to solitary monologue, Husserl is also cutting off language from its relation to the world. Derrida does not recognise that according to Husserl even solitary monologue is *about* the world. It still has, not only meaning, but also reference. See J. Derrida, *Speech and Phenomena*, E. Tr. by D. Allison. Evanston: Northwestern University Press, 1973.

[2] *Ideas*, I, § 124.

[3] Cp. Heinz Hülsmann, *Zur Theorie der Sprache bei Edmund Husserl*. München: Verlag Anton Pustel, 1964, esp. pp. 240–241.

inner, *Sprachlichkeit* survives as in solitary phantasised monologue.

Compare with the Husserlian move, the following account by
Findlay of Hegel's remarks on language in the *Encyclopädie*
(§459): "... Hegel prefers the *pure* sign to the sign that is pictorial
or hieroglyphic as affording a greater mental liberation. He also
prefers the short-lived spirituality of the spoken, to the long-lived
fixity of the written, word. A further step in the mastery occurs
when the word is itself "internalized" and becomes a private image:
... Here the mind can at last discourse with itself in signs that
have the clear fixity and lastingness of what is outward, while
they also have the ready manipulability of what is subjective and
inward."[1]

Hegel's remarks here about language belong to the section on
Subjective Spirit whose one-sidedness, within the Hegelian system, has to be remedied by transition to Objective Spirit. Husserl's return to the monologue is likewise a move that has to be
supplemented by the thesis of the ideal objectivity of meanings
and by the later thesis about the ideality of the linguistic as such[2]
and the intersubjective constitution of language as a *Kulturgebil-
de*.[3] How are these aspects to be related to each other? Derrida
finds the reduction to the inner phantasised speech and the thesis
of the ideality of meanings as being of a piece, and speaks of the
'illicit complicity' between voice and ideality.[4] One would have
expected that with the shift of emphasis from the written language
to the spoken, from the spoken to the act of speaking, the decisive
step had been taken, that would put meanings back in the living
context of acts. What Derrida possibly means by the 'complicity'
may be that ideality of the object requires that the consciousness
of that object should be non-empirical and that the disembodied,
inner phantasised voice precisely is that non-empirical consciousness. Now Husserl's thesis is not that a non-empirical consciousness is needed for having an ideal meaning for its correlate, but
rather that real, temporal acts of consciousness are correlated to

   ³ J. N. Findlay, *Hegel: A Re-Examination*. New York: Collier, 1962, p. 307. Hegel
also writes in *Encyclopädie*, § 457: "Die Phantasie ist der Mittelpunkt, in welchem
das Allgemeine und das Sein, das Eigene und das Gefundensein, das Innere und Äus-
sere vollkommen in eins geschaffen sind."

   ¹ *Formale und transzendentale Logik*.

   ² See esp. *Phänomenologische Psychologie* (Husserliana IX), Beilage IX.

   ³ Derrida, *Speech and Phenomena*, p. 77.

ideal meanings.[1] The inner phantasised speech is as much a real temporal event as the overt speech: in no case is the act repeatable while in every case the 'ideal content' of the act is.

IV

The theory of meaning of the first Investigation is subsequently extended by Husserl, as is well known, to all intentional acts. This extension and its implications were not treated by me in the book, and it is only appropriate that some remarks on it be made at this point. The problem of meaning appears to have its original locus in the act of speaking, and it seems odd that Husserl would have spoken of meanings of such acts as perceiving, imagining, remembering, thinking, and also of hoping, desiring, loving, hating, giving orders or asking questions. And yet a deep-lying structure of Husserlian thinking would remain obscure unless and until we are able to appreciate the nature of this extension, for which the basic text is the following passage from the *Ideas I*: "Originally these words (*'Bedeutung'* and *'Bedeuten'*) relate only to the sphere of speech, that of "expression". But it is almost inevitable, and at the same time an important step for knowledge, to extend the meaning of these words, and to modify them suitably so that they may be applied in a certain way to the whole noetico-noematic sphere, to all acts, therefore, whether these are interwoven with expressions or not."[2]

And for thus extended concept of meaning Husserl prefers to use the word *'Sinn'* – retaining the word *'Bedeutung'* for meaning of expressions, for meaning at the conceptual level.[3]

Now there is one way of interpreting this move that is, in my opinion, wrong. From the fact that Husserl seems to extend the concept of 'linguistic meaning' to all acts, together with the fact that according to him "whatever is "meant as such", every meaning (*Meinung*) in the noematic sense ... of any act whatsoever *can be expressed* conceptually (durch "bedeutungen,")"[4] it might seem that the Husserlian noema is nothing but the 'lin-

---

[1] Cp. A. Gurwitsch, *Studies in Phenomenology and Psychology*. Evanston: Northwestern University Press, 1966, pp. 156–157.

[2] *Ideas*, I, § 124.

[3] *Ideas*, I, § 124.

[4] *Ideas*, I, § 124.

guistic meaning' – that to ascertain the noema of an act we need but to ascertain the 'linguistic meaning' of the expression that verbalizes that act.[1] Such an interpretation no doubt places at our disposal a more readily and tangibly manipulable meaning of 'Sinn', but gains that advantage at the risk of missing something essential to that Husserlian notion. Husserl says that every act is expressible, that "expression" is "a remarkable form, which permits of being adapted to every "meaning" (to the noematic "nucleus"), and raises it to the realm of the "Logos", of the *conceptual*, and therewith of the "general"."[2] He also says that "expressing" indicates a special act stratum. The relation of this act-stratum to other non-linguistic acts is sought to be illuminated by such metaphors as 'blending', 'adapting', 'adapting', 'mirroring' and 'copying', although he also warns us against the risk of such figures of speech. He goes on to raise questions such as these: how to interpret the idea of expressing what is expressed? How are the expressed acts related to those that are not expressed? What modification does the act of expressing introduce into the structure of the original pre-expressive act? We are then told that the expressive act is not 'productive', that it carries over, while only giving a conceptual form, the sense as well as the positionality of the original act. There is thus a pre-conceptual sense which is not fully captured by the conceptual form: "the upper layer need not extend its expressing function over the entire lower layer."[3] Not only it need not be entirely congruent, it is bound to suffer from a certain incompleteness owing to the generality which excludes many specifications and variabilities. Thus identity is ruled out and a close connection, even a limited congruence, is recognised. For logical purposes, linguistic, conceptual meaning is what matters; for phenomenological purposes, it has to be placed in the context of the richer non-linguistic meaning.

It hardly needs to be added, after what has been said earlier, that for Husserl there is nothing, strictly speaking, like what is called 'linguistic meaning.' The meaning of expressions is at bottom the sense of the acts of expressing: a point which was pointed out to be a basic difference from Frege's concept of *Sinn*.

There are two opposed ways of looking at what Husserl is

---

[1] This seems to be the position of Smith and McIntyre.
[2] *Ideas*, I, § 124.
[3] *Ideas*, I, § 126.

doing. One may hold that he is (wrongly) applying the perceptual model to linguistic meaning, as though for him to meaningfully use an expression or to understand one is to intuit the appropriate meanings, have them before the mental gaze. Or, one may hold that in extending a concept of meaning derived from phenomenology of speaking to pre-linguistic acts Husserl is (wrongly) applying the model of conceptual thinking to perceptual, intuitive, as also other non-objectivating acts. The deeper nature of Husserlian thinking lies in the fact that *both* these models are plausible, that it is possible to look at the total situation from *both* these points of view. The perceptual model was no doubt very much in Husserl's mind. But the meaning conferring act was also regarded as an 'interpretative' act. If in the case of perception one may say that sensations are 'interpreted' to signify such and such perceptual object, one may also say that in the experience of meanings inscriptions or sounds are 'interpreted' to signify such and such meanings.[1] In relation to the perceptual object, the act of perceiving is a 'presentation', but in relation to the sensory data it is an 'interpretation.' Similarly, in the case of meanings my act of understanding is both an intuitive grasp and an act of interpreting. Thus hermeneutic phenomenology finds its rightful place within the structure of Husserlian thought. The interpretative model – not to speak of the still narrower model of text-interpretation – finds its proper limits in the intuitive. They do neatly divide the total realm of experience amongst themselves, but thoroughly interpenetrate and coexist with each other.

Nevertheless, there is a certain universality, for Husserl, of the linguistic act. Speaking is a mode of consciousness, but it has a universality which does not belong to any other. This is implied in the thesis that the sense of every act is expressible. This essential expressibility of all acts as also the mutual adaptability of pre-expressive and expressive acts suggest that in speech the domain of consciousness is, as though, mapped onto itself. Speech act is not primordial, for it presupposes pre-linguistic acts. But it is universal in the sense that, of all other modes of consciousness, it permits the entire domain of consciousness to be mapped onto itself. Mute consciousness can be brought to speech. Phenomenology as a science rests on this possibility.

---

[1] LI, I, pp. 310, 365; II, p. 568.

V

Husserlian semantics has, besides its theory of meaning, a theory of reference. Here again Husserl's theory differs from Frege's not only with regard to the reference of sentences (which, according to Frege is its truth-value and according to Husserl the fact stated by it) but also (i) with regard to the reference of predicates and (ii) reference of names within intensional contexts. As early as 1891, in a letter to Husserl, Frege distinguished between his own theory of reference of concept words and Husserl's thus: on Husserl's theory, the sense of a concept word is the concept and the reference is the object or objects which fall under the concept; on Frege's theory, the concept word has a sense which is other than the concept, the concept is rather its reference. Frege then continues: "In the case of concept words, one more step is needed than in the case of proper names in order to reach the object, and this last may be missing – i.e. the concept may be empty, without the concept word ceasing thereby to be scientifically applicable."[1] An empty concept word, Frege wants to say, does not lack reference, it refers to a concept; it is empty because there are no objects falling under that concept. Frege's problem – or rather, the problem for Frege exegesis – is: what does he want to count as the sense of the concept word?[2] There is the additional problem that if a concept is a referent, it becomes an object of some sort, which is ill consistent with his distinction between object and concept.[3] Husserl's view, which is the more traditional one, is that the concept is the meaning of the concept word and the objects falling under the concept constitute its reference. But what is the reference of the predicate 'a horse' in 'Bucephalus is a horse'? One may construe 'Bucephalus is a horse' as 'Bucephalus = a horse' in order to show that 'a horse' refers to the same thing that is designated by 'Bucephalus'. But this would reduce the predicate to a name. We are also, in such a con-

[1] See "Frege-Husserl Correspondence".

[2] Contrast the interpretation of Wm. Marshall (who wants to say that in the case of predicates Frege would not distinguish between 'sense' and 'reference') with that of M. Dummett. See E. D. Klemke (ed), *Essays on Frege*. University of Illinois Press, 1968.

[3] Klemke suggests the use of the word "entity" to include both objects and concepts. see *Essays on Frege*, p. 158–160.

struction, left with the predicate 'identical with a horse' and would want to know what *its* reference is. Searl has argued that 'if Bucephalus is not a horse' is given a similar construction ('Bucephalus is not identical with a horse'), one may very well ask, 'Which horse?'.[1] Husserl does not follow this route to give the reference of 'a horse'. The expression 'a horse' has rather an indefiniteness which gives it an 'extension', i.e. a range of possible application; in the case of predicates, the range is explicated by "the logical possibility of propositions of a certain sort."[2] Thus the sense in which a predicate is 'about' something is somewhat different from the case of names. In the *Formale und Transzendentale Logik*, Husserl writes that the predicate 'is white' (in 'This paper is white') goes beyond its own *Sachbezüglichkeit* and comprehends within its own that of the subject term.[3] What he appears to mean is that the indefinite range of extension of the predicate is made definite by the reference of the subject term. It is not as though Husserl is treating the predicate expression as a name. He recognises the syntactic difference between names and predicates as well as the difference between the two kinds of speech acts: naming and predicating. Only, he holds that both names and predicates refer, that the extra-linguistic reference of an entire sentence is 'founded' on the references of its two components. He also thinks that, in a strict sense, an object is what can be named, and allows that every expression can be nominalised. But at the same time, we have to bear in mind that the nominalised expression refers to a new object, and not to the object referred to by the original expression.

The entire declarative sentence refers to a fact (*Sachlage*), though it may also be said to be *about* that which is referred to by the subject term. One should then distinguish between the *Gegenstandsworüber*, that-about-which of a propositional act, or also its substrate and the objective correlate of that act. In the statement 'The paper is white', the paper is what the statement is about, the fact that the paper is white is what is being stated, but the fact stated is not being 'presented' or named. The many-rayed synthetic positing act of judging is different from the single rayed act of presentation. One must then distinguish between uttering

---

[1] J. Searls, *Speech Acts*. Cambridge: Cambridge University Press, p. 27. 1969.
[2] LI, I, 372.
[3] *Formale und transzendentale Logik*, Beilage I.

a sentence, saying something about something by that utterance, asserting a proposition, stating a fact, naming the fact so stated, naming the proposition asserted, and naming the sentence uttered.

Husserl's conception of the reference of a declarative sentence is further complicated by a distinction between *Sachlage* and *Sachverhalt*. He says that 'a > b' and 'b < a' refer to the same *Sachlage*.[1] In *Experience and Judgment* § 59 he writes that an identical *Sachlage* can be explicated into many predicative *Sachverhalten*. If the fact stated by a sentence is what makes that sentence true, then the fact stated by 'a > b' and 'b < a' is the same: fact, in this sense, is the *Sachlage*. But each such *Sachlage* founds the possibility of many *Sachverhalten*. Each such *Sachverhalt* is a syntactical objectivity constituted by a predicative act and is the objective correlate of that act. The expression 'The fact that a > b' names, by objectifying, such a *Sachverhalt*.

We may then say that the statement 'This paper is white' is *about* the piece of paper designated by 'This paper', *states* the *Sachlage* which is receptively constituted by pre-predicative explication, and has as its *correlate* a syntactical objectivity, a *Sachverhalt*, that is *named* by 'The fact that this paper is white.'

Thus, two sentences with different meanings must have different *Sachverhalten* as their correlates, but may refer to one and the same *Sachlage*. But this gives rise to the question: how is *Sachverhalt* related to the proposition or meaning expressed by a sentence? In *Experience and Judgment* § 69, Husserl gives his answer: one should distinguish between the *actual Sachverhalt* and the *Sachverhalt* supposed as such, the latter is the proposition, the actual *Sachverhalt* being the objectified propositional meaning.[2] The former, i.e. the *Sachverhalt itself* is the idea of the complete confirmation of the presumption of *Sachverhalt*. With this one sees a certain difference between the conception of reference as applied to names and as applied to sentences.[3] A name never names its own meaning (according to Husserl, though for Frege it does so in act and oblique contexts), while the reference of a sentence, in one sense, is nothing but its objectified meaning. However, there are two other senses in which the reference of a

---

[1] LI, I, p. 288.
[2] See R. Sokolowski, *Husserlian Meditations*, pp. 45–47, 52–53.
[3] J. Searls, *Speech Acts*, *p*.

sentence is other than its meaning: neither the *Gegenstandworüber* nor the *Sachlage* it states is its meaning objectified.

To these remarks, I should add one more in connection with Husserl's theory of reference. There is a concept of reference – which in fact is the prevailing concept – according to which if an expression, or an occurence of it, refers, then there must exist that to which it refers.[1] Now this certainly is not Husserl's concept of referring. 'Referring' is an intentional concept, to say that an expression refers to an object does not entail the existence of that object. What then is constitutive of an expression, or of the speech act expressed in it, is the intention to refer, not reference construed as a real relation between two reals, the word and the thing. This partly accounts for the fact that Husserl's semantics does not need a theory like Frege's according to which names refer, in act and oblique contexts, to their customary senses. This theory lacks intuitive support. One who believes that Brutus killed Caeser does not believe in a relationship amongst the meanings of the names and predicate words involved.[2]

VI

There are two strands of thought in Husserl's philosophy. Phenomenology began as a program of describing, on the basis of intuitive testimony, *essences* and essential structures of various regions of phenomena. But it was also concerned with *meanings*, and gradually the concern with meanings, the enterprise of clarification and genesis of meanings, overshadowed the other, i.e. the essentialism. For a time, 'meaning' and 'essence' were identified (as in *Logical Investigations*, I, p. 330), but the two came to be sharply distinguished (as in *Experience and Judgment*, § 64 d). 'Essence' remained an ontological concept. 'Meaning' is at first a semantic, but then a phenomenological concept. Both designate intensional entities, but 'meaning', and not 'essence', is tied to the concept of intentionality. To be is to be a possible object of reference. Any entity that we admit into our ontology must be such that it can be referred to. Real individuals as well as essences can be referred to. Meanings are not objects of reference, but media for reference. Frege's *Sinne* are members of Frege's ontology, they

---

[1] J. Searls, *Speech Acts*, p.
[2] McIntyre shows this very convincingly in his dissertation.

are objects of reference in oblique contexts. But Husserl's meanings are not members of his ontology, essences are. Meanings are
isolated in a phenomenological attitude, via reductions and epoche,
which turns away from the object oriented, naively ontological
point of view. The transition is analogous to Quine's 'semantic
ascent'.[1] First-order language is ontologically oriented, it is about
the world. Phenomenological 'ascent', if we can speak of it in that
manner, reveals ontological committments in their true character,
i.e. as committments, predicates that were regarded in the material mode are now seen to be meanings constituted in appropriate
acts.

   What does Husserlian phenomenology mean by 'clarification of
meaning'? I will here draw attention to two features of this enterprise by contrasting it, on the one hand, with the method prac-
tised by the Wittgensteinian analysts and on the other with a
very different procedure followed by Hegel in his *Phenomenology
of Mind*. The philosophers who follow the later Wittgenstein seek
to clarify meanings by focusing on how we use the appropriate
words, i.e. by locating the appropriate words within the relevant
language game. On such a view, to lay bare how a word is used is
not by any means on the part of the user or users of the language
to introspect and look into their own minds, but to observe a
language game as a publicly observable social phenomenon. Once
the relevant language game has been brought to light, the implicit
rules have been made explicit, the permissible moves have been
kept apart from the not permissible ones, we would have done all
that is necessary by way of clarification. Although Husserl does
not agree that the nature of linguistic activity can be correctly
captured by the metaphor of playing games, he yet does assign
a priority to speech *act* over language as a *system*. Meanings then
have to be clarified by returning to the acts. But again speech
act is not merely a sort of rule governed behavior, but essentially
an intentional act. Speaking is a mode of consciousness, while at
the same time, it has – as pointed out earlier – a certain universality. It is this consciousness of speaking with its noetic and
noematic structure which Husserl wants to describe.

   Contrasting with Hegel, in whom there is an analogous transition from essence to concept, one notes a fundamental difference

---

[1] W. V. O. Quine, *Word and Object*. Cambridge: M.I.T. Press, p. 271.

in motivation. Hegel's reflections in the *Phenomenology*, or even
in the *Logic*, are intended to bring out the *truth* of the reflected-
upon. The series of forms of consciousness which Hegel presents
is so ordered that every succeeding member is the truth of the
preceeding. The series has a closure in Absolute Knowledge. In
Husserlian phenomenology there is not such hierarchy, no closure, no Absolute Knowledge, no condemnation of a form of consciousness as 'lower'. This difference in structure is due to the
fact that Husserlian phenomenology, in its search for meanings,
is guided by *respect* for the given. All clarification and constitution
analysis of meanings must follow the guiding clue provided by the
given sense. It does not question the given in order to bring to
light where it goes wrong, it questions it in order to discover what
it further implies. It does not judge, but seeks to understand.
Hegelian phenomenology, in its search for the truth, suspects
the given sense. Its *suspicion* leads to the question: is a form
of consciousness (say, perception) really what it thinks itself to
be? In fact, for Hegel, there is a difference between what a
form of consciousness in fact is and what it thinks itself to be.
It does not accept on trust the initial report of the naive
consciousness. It seeks to go deeper and to decipher what is its
truth. Husserlian phenomenology cannot question the veracity of
the given noematic sense, it can only undertake to clarify this
sense by returning to the acts in which it is constituted. Philosophy shall not revise our categories, but shall describe both the
surface and deep structures. Hegelian phenomenology ends up by
being a revisionary metaphysics. The *epoché* is not an expression
of suspicion in the veracity of the given, it is rather a methodol-
ogical step needed for understanding the sense of the world
precisely as it is given, i.e. as a unity of sense that is achieved.

This contrast between philosophy as the search for truth and
as pursuit of meanings with a view to clarify them is important
for understanding the complex motivations of Husserl's thinking.
When in the *Krisis*, the objective sciences are traced back to the
life-world, we are said to reach the *Sinnesfundament*, the foundation of meaning of the sciences – but not their truth. This also
helps us to appreciate the true role of the concept of Transcendental Subjectivity in Husserlian thought, but that is a theme
which this Introduction will not venture to touch upon.

VII

There is one criticism of Husserlian thinking about meaning which I want to recall here – a criticism which was implicit in many of my comments in the book. In connection with 'occasional expressions', it was maintained that the distinction between 'theoretical' and 'practical' expressions is irreducible, that the attempt of Husserl to replace occasional expressions, in an ideal language, by expressions having general meanings is misconceived. A similar criticism was made against Husserl's theory that what is *expressed* in an interrogative or imperative sentence is not the living questioning or the living act of giving an order, but rather an inner perception of these non-objectifying acts. Now these detached comments were part of an over all, though implicit, criticism which may now be formulated thus: Husserlian theory of meaning is a theory of *theoretical* meaning. This is understandable in the case of a theory which takes its start with reflections on the nature of logic and mathematics. In the *Prolegomena*, Husserl's conception of theory is narrowly limited to deductive, nomological structures. With the gradual coming into prominence of the so-called 'sciences of the mind', possibly under the influence of his contacts with Dilthey, the conception of 'science' and that of 'theory' are broadened. But Husserl's orientation is still theoretical. In philosophy of language, his central concern is with theoretical discourse. His theory of ideality of meanings suits this discourse. Other forms of discourse, practical and poetic, fall outside its scope. But Husserl, with a claim to universality of his theory, wants to subsume those non-theoretical forms of discourse also within it.

Now faced with such a fundamental criticism, Husserl's response may be as follows. It is no doubt true that theoretical discourse is not the primordial form of discourse, that theory and science have their origin in pre-theoretical forms of the life world. Theoretical discourse is one possibility, not the only one. But philosophy itself, and so also phenomenology, is theory. Either one does not philosophise and is engaged in the act of living, or one does philosophise. In the latter case, one is theorising. It is inevitable then that a theory of meaning would be prejudiced in favor of the theoretical. But this is really not a matter of prejudice, nor

is the consequence trivial. Husserl is guided by the insight that
every act, objectifying or not, contains within its structure a
component that is objectifying. "Every consciousness is either
actually or potentially "thetic"." "Every act, as also every act-
correlate, harbours explicitly or implicitly a "logical" factor."[1]
In fact, all *expressing* is a doxic act.[2] This partly explains Husserl's continuing concern with logic even when he was doing
transcendental phenomenology. For him, the theoretical and the
specifically logical pervades all human experience, the entire
domain of intentionality. Thus the distinction between the theoretical and the practical is, for him, a distinction *within the theoretical*. Whereas for many thinkers theory itself is a form of practice, disinterestedness itself is a form of interest, for Husserl – it
would seem – the practical is a nascent theory, the life-world a
proto-logical structure, within the interest that ties us to the world
of action and affection there are germs for that detachment, disin-
terest and objectification which characterise theory in various
degrees. He can account for the fact that science and philosophy
should be able to take their birth out of the life of interest. He
cannot account for that discontinuity which looms large between
these two forms of life. The other group of philosophers with whom
we have contrasted Husserl are no better off in either respect. One
may add that this universality of theory is closely tied, in Husserl's
thought, with the idea of transcendental subjectivity. How precisely the three central concerns of his philosophy hang together
– essence, meaning and transcendental subjectivity – I will not
seek to discuss here.

VIII

The concern with meanings characterises a large segment of
contemporary philosophy. Husserl's philosophy of meaning,
when compared with many others, is distinguished by its com-
prehensiveness, by its perceptiveness to the many-sided nature
of our commerce with meanings. Most theories begin with prejudices, metaphysical or epistemological. One such prejudice is that
against the inner and the mental and in favor of the outer and
the public. There is the correlated epistemological prejudice in

[1] *Ideas*, I, § 117.
[2] *Ibid*, § 127.

favor of public verifiability as a criterion of significance. Critics of the concept of meaning such as Quine begin with pre-conceptions about the nature of philosophy (as continuous with science), and about the nature of science (as truth-functional and extensional). Husserlian philosophy does not need such pre-conceptions. Furthermore, theories of meaning either take into account the intention of the speaker or do not; they are either Platonistic or anti-Platonistic. The Platonistic theories are in a better position in accounting for the identity, objectivity and communicability of meanings. They err by hypostatising them. The psychological theories have the advantage of not severing meanings from the mental life of persons; but they do not have the concept of intentionality which alone could rescue meanings from the privacy of one's mental life. The theories which emphasize the centrality of the speaker's intention ('S intends to mean m by uttering 'e'') remain at the level of communicative speech. The rule theory knows only what Husserl calls 'game meaning' of signs which presupposes, by doing duty for, the original conceptual meaning.[1] It does not ask, what sort of intentional act is 'using' or 'making a move according to rules', and what its noematic correlate is, and how this transformation of the original act of speaking constitutes a new noematic sense. As a purely descriptive theory, Husserl's theory does not suffer by contrast with any other prevailing theory of meaning.

Graduate Faculty,   J. N. Mohanty
New School for Social Research,
New York

---

[1] LI, I, p. 305.

CHAPTER I

ANALYSIS OF THOUGHT

§ I. There is one dominating interest which runs through all the works of Husserl, from the earliest to the latest, and imparts to his philosophical career an almost tragic note: this is the search for a stable *via media* between Platonism and Anti-Platonism. Those who, following a well-known pattern, divide his philosophical works into the early psychological period of the *Philosophie der Arithmetik*, a middle Platonic period of the first volume of the *Logische Untersuchungen*, and a concluding idealistic phase beginning with the second volume of the *Logische Untersuchungen* and the *Ideen*, introduce a division which is too rigid to permit a correct appreciation of that equilibrium which Husserl was unceasingly seeking for. This search renders any demarcation of the phases impossible. The present work is not intended to be a study of the development of Husserl's thought; it is also not intended to cover the entire range of his philosophical thought. The immediate purpose of this study is to bring out exactly those points in Husserl's philosophy which are relevant to contemporary discussions of the problems of language, thought, meaning and experience. These points are varied in nature and importance, but all through, as we shall have occasions to show, Husserl attempts to steer clear of the two extremes of Platonism and Anti-Platonism. It is the conviction underlying the present work that such an approach has a direct bearing upon the contemporary preoccupation with the value and validity of Platonism in epistemology and ontology. One contemporary philosopher has cautioned us against Plato's beard, while another has spoken of Plato's ghost as always lurking behind the corner; White,[1] in an engaging study, has crusaded against all forms of Platonism and has heightened our awareness

[1] M. White, *Reunion in Philosophy*, Harvard, 1956.

of the very subtle manner in which Platonism has a tendency to reassert itself. This contemporary Anti-Platonism contrasts well with the professed Platonism of the first decades of this century, the Platonism of Russell and Moore, Whitehead and Santayana. One of the major issues of modern philosophy could then be defined in the language of Platonism *vis-à-vis* Anti-Platonism. It is against this background of contemporary scene that we shall turn to Husserl.

There is at least one reason that makes a study of Husserl particularly interesting. He is one of the very few amongst the preanalytical philosophers who refuse to be classified by any 'ism.' In fact, his peculiar method enabled him to combine in his philosophy elements as diverse as 'realism' and 'idealism,' 'rationalism' and 'empiricism,' 'positivism' and 'pragmatism,' 'intuitionism' and 'intellectualism.' It is indeed an interesting task to distinguish between these different strands of his thought. It is possible that one would then come to realise that these elements are not as incompatible with each other as they appear to be as soon as they are designated by the various 'ism's. Free them from the crusading labels, rescue them from the claims and counterclaims of theories, and they would prove themselves to be valuable philosophical findings, neutral as against rival theories.

§ 2. The background of the contemporary philosophical scene which we have set for this study makes it most appropriate that we should begin with Husserl's philosophy of language. But, as is unavoidable, in expounding his philosophy of language, we shall be led on to his theory of meaning which is the subject matter of the following chapters. Our interest in language again derives from the interest in studying the nature of human thinking; it would be appropriate therefore to begin with an analysis of human thinking. Such an analysis, it is needless to say, could only be provisional at this stage; for the ensuing discussions would be fruitless unless they served to substantiate and explicate it to some appreciable extent.

A five-membered analysis of thought may be good enough to start with. And then it may be safe to examine the claim of each one of these five to have a place in a satisfactory philosophy of thought. These five are:

(a) the thinking subject;

(b) the thinking process, i.e., thinking as a real, temporal, psychological process;

(c) the thought itself;

(d) the linguistic expression;

and (e) the object of thought.

The factor (a) is the thinker himself, for there must be some one who thinks. The distinction between (b) and (c) is a basic distinction for all analysis of thought. (b) refers to the process of thinking, as it happens in the thinker's mind, as it forms one of the topics for the psychologists to study and as it could be introspectively observed only by the thinker himself; (c) refers to the objective, over-individual content of the subjective, individual thinking. Unless (c) be admitted into our analysis, there seems to be no possibility of explaining the objectivity, communicability and sharability of thoughts. No analysis of thought could dispute the presence of (d), even if there could very well be differences of opinion regarding the function and importance of this factor. A generalised distinction between (c) and (e) is difficult to draw, but the one that immediately suggests itself to us is Frege's well-known distinction between *Sinn* and *Bedeutung*.

As against the above five-membered analysis, Husserl gives us a three-membered one in which (a) is totally dropped and (b) as a psychological process is also dispensed with. Husserl's analysis therefore recognises the following three factors:

(á) the linguistic expression;

(b') the thinking;

and (ć) the thought.

According to this latter analysis, (a) and (b) are irrelevant to any logical study of thought. For the understanding of a person's thought, it is of course irrelevant who thinks and what is happening in his mind. The only relevant factors are: the linguistic expression and the thought i.e. the objective meaning expressed. If I judge '2 is the only even prime number,' the understanding of my judgment requires hearing or seeing the symbols I use, understanding their meaning, and understanding what I am talking about. It is quite irrelevant who I am that judges and what has been happening in my mind as I so judged.

Without labouring this point any further, it may be added that Husserl's philosophy of thought is not concerned with the psychological question – what happens in the mind when one thinks? – which an Aristotelian Society symposium [1] sought to investigate. It is needless therefore to add that (b') of the Husserlian scheme is not quite the same as (b) of the five-membered analysis. Nor is (ċ) just the same as (c). One way of bringing out the difference between (ċ) and (c) is to show the different relations in which they stand to (b') and (b) respectively. In the philosophies that subscribe to the first type of analysis, (c) is the ideal-objective content which is discovered, arrived at, grasped etc. by the psychological process (b). In Husserl's philosophy the relation between (ċ) and (b') is not as external as that; (b') has not the simple function of discovering, or leading upto (ċ). On the other hand, (ċ) and (b') are two inseparable aspects of one experience, (b') being, in Husserl's language, the meaning-conferring or meaning-constituting experience and (ċ) the constituted meaning itself. These two notions would be clarified in the course of the present study. In the meantime, it should be stressed that by establishing an inseparable relationship between (b') and (ċ), Husserl escapes the charge of having hypostatized meanings, i.e., of turning them into rigid entities. It is (c) in the first scheme and (ċ) in the Husserlian scheme that are the bugbear of the modern anti-Platonists. White,[2] for example, while expounding Russell's early Platonism, makes it centre round the argument that in thought we 'grasp' or 'apprehend' an objective meaning. In doing this, White is ascribing to Russell an analysis of the first type. The status of (ċ) in Husserl's philosophy is not as simply characterizable as that. At the risk of a paradox, and with the hope of being able to substantiate in the later chapters what I say now, let me suggest that according to Husserl, we *both create and grasp* meanings. To see through this paradox is also to appreciate the sort of equilibrium Husserl tried to maintain between the extremes of Platonism and Anti-Platonism.

[1] *Proceedings of the Aristotelian Society*, Suppl., Vol. 25, 1951.
[2] *loc. cit.*, p. 38.

At this stage of our provisional exposition, one may have to encounter the objection that an analysis of thought with the help of (á) alone being possible, both (b') and (ć) are superfluous and therefore should be struck off the list. This, I should think, is the implication of the theory defended by Ayer in his *Thinking and Meaning*.[1] To think is to manipulate symbols according to rules; meaning belongs to symbols by virtue of the rules laid down in the language-system concerned. There is no process of thinking *in addition to* the operation with symbols; there is also no *thought* that is expressed through the symbols.

To be able to defend Husserl against the above objection which may be raised by this modern, and very influential, school of philosophy, ably represented by Ayer, it is necessary to go into Husserl's philosophy of language and meaning. For it is only by examining the nature of linguistic symbolization and the way expressions mean that we can truly evaluate the sort of theory proposed by Ayer and others.

§ 3. Ayer's theory may be called the *operational theory* of thinking because of the fact that it reduces thinking to operation with symbols. It must not in any case be confused with what Price has called the *Sign theory*.[2] The operational theory is free from the behaviouristic character of the Sign theory. A detailed criticism of the Sign theory is not called for. Nevertheless, a few critical remarks would not be out of order before we lay it aside.

The Sign theory does not recognize any fundamental distinction between linguistic expressions and other natural or artificial signs: they all are taken to *mean* in the same way, i.e., by evoking appropriate responses and behaviour-patterns. Price has raised two pertinent objections against this theory. In the first place, the theory involves a vicious circle; for, if to understand an expression is to know what responses to make, to know what responses to make should as well presuppose an understanding of the expression concerned. This circularity points to the fact that an expression is not, to start with, an unmeaning sign and gathers meaning only when we have learnt the appropriate behaviour-pattern, but that it is from the very

[1] A. J. Ayer, *Thinking and Meaning*, London, 1947.
[2] H. H. Price, *Thinking and Experience*, London, 1953, Ch. VI.

beginning, in so far as it is an expression, a meaningful sign. It is only our prior understanding which explains the appropriateness of the behaviour-pattern. Secondly, the Sign theory according to Price views the situation from the consumer's end and not from the producer's.[1]

We could improve upon this last valuable suggestion in the following way. Let us take a situation in which one person utters meaningful expressions and another person hears him and also understands what he says. The speaker, in such a situation, is the producer; the hearer is the consumer. The nature of thought could be studied from three different points of view, namely the points of view of the speaker, the hearer and an onlooker. By the onlooker, we mean any other person, including the psychologist, who observes the speaker and the hearer as involved in a situation like the one imagined here. Now, Price seems to be suggesting that the Sign theory, and for that reason any behaviouristic account of thinking, is based on the consumer's, that is to say, the hearer's standpoint. It would perhaps be more appropriate to say that the Sign theory is based on the standpoint of the onlooker; it does justice neither to the experience of the speaker, nor to the experience of the hearer, i.e. of him who receives communication, but only to the experience of the external observer who is *observing* what is *happening*. There is no doubt an apparent plausibility in referring the Sign theory to the consumer's standpoint, for it is the hearer whom we find responding appropriately to the stimulus received. But it is as onlookers that *we* observe this. The hearer no doubt behaves appropriately, but his *understanding*, as *he* experiences it, is not the same as his behaving in a certain way. We conclude therefore that the Sign theory of thinking has its origin in the standpoint of the onlooker; one such onlooker is the behaviourist psychologist engaged in observing the stimulus-response situation in which the speaker and the hearer are involved.

Having pointed out these basic differences in approach to the problem of thought and understanding, we could even go ahead and suggest that a theory which is formulated *exclusively* from the point of view of the producer, i.e. of the thinker, is also doomed to failure. One such theory is the much discussed, and

[1] H. H. Price, *loc. cit.*, p. 198.

fortunately now almost abandoned, *Image theory* of thinking.
The image theory takes up the exclusive standpoint of the
producer, the thinker; its basic question is: what is happening
in the mind of the person who is thinking? Psychological intro-
spection reveals nothing but images. We need not linger on this
theory. Much has been said against it. Recently, Wittgenstein
has dealt a deathblow to the theory that understanding consists
in having introspectible mental experiences.[1] Borrowing Price's
metaphor, we may suggest that unless the goods produced are
fit to be consumed, we do not even have a genuine producer. If
what the thinker produces are images that are intrinsically
incapable of being communicated and therefore with regard to
which the question of consumption is *ab initio* ruled out, there
is no consumer, and strictly speaking, also no producer. This
points to the fact that a true philosophy of thought should in-
stall itself in a position midway between the producer and the
consumer, and should yet remain internal to both. It is impossible
to separate the standpoints of the producer and the consumer
without doing violence to the phenomenon of thought and its
communication. Once *this peculiarly philosophical* standpoint
is adopted it would be realised that understanding is neither
behaving appropriately, nor undergoing certain psychological
experiences like having images. What is it then?

The operational theory answers by saying that thinking
consists in operating with symbols according to the accepted
rules. This theory, it hardly needs to be mentioned, can be made
free from the behaviouristic attachments which unavoidably
vitiate the Sign theory; and, of course, it *is* free from the psychologism of the Image theory. With a view to undertaking a
proper evaluation of this theory, we shall introduce in the next
chapter certain fundamental distinctions drawn by Husserl.

---

[1] Cfr. L. Wittgenstein, *Philosophical Investigations*, Oxford, 1953, especially
pp. 54–56.

CHAPTER II

EXPRESSION AND ITS FUNCTIONS

§ 4. To be a sign [1] is to be a sign for something. To be a sign for something is to point it out. But not all signs exercise an additional function of meaning, or giving expression to a meaning. In other words, not all signs are expressions. The concept of sign is wider than the concept of expression, for expressions are *also* signs inasmuch as the functions of signifying and meaning are interlaced in them. This does not imply, Husserl warns us, that the *function* of meaning is a species of the *function* of signifying or pointing out. Though expressions constitute a species of signs, to mean is not a sort of pointing out. The two are *totally* different functions.

Let us call those signs 'marks', that only point out but do not also mean. Signs, therefore, are either marks or expressions. Marks again may be of different kinds. For example, the way in which a flag is the mark of a nation is different from the way in which the canals on Mars are the marks of the existence of intelligent inhabitants. Husserl, however, lays great emphasis on the point that a mark, as a mere mark, does not require any insight into its connection with that for which it is a sign.[2] When we say that A is a mark of B, we are not contending that there is any rational necessity about this relation between A and B. What happens is that my belief in the existence of A is *experienced as motive* for believing in the existence of B. The fact that such *motivation* is not insightful serves to distinguish the function of pointing to... from the function of proving that... Without being insightful, the motivation experienced in the case of a sign may yet be free from all doubt and may amount to an absolute certainty about B. Husserl does not object to the doctrine that

---

[1] *L.U.*, II, 1, First Investigation, Ch. I.
[2] *L.U.*, II, 1, p. 25 f.

the relation between the sign and the signified is a product of association of ideas; he only reminds us that the function of the association of ideas should not be confined to a mere reproduction of past experiences. The association may also be said to be genuinely creative in the sense that the sign and the signified are made to enter into a new unity that cannot be detected in the original contents of both. When A calls B to our mind, what we find is *not merely* that A and B are experienced together or one after the other, but also that there subsists between them *a felt unity*. Association, therefore, is productive in so far as it welds the two different things into a felt unity. Subject to this reservation, Husserl accepts the theory that A comes to be the sign of B through association of ideas. It should however be remembered that the felt unity which binds the sign with the signified is not a rational or logical connection; it is a merely felt unity, though nevertheless a unity.

4.1.   Expressions are meaningful signs. In this sense of the term, speech or parts of speech are expressions, though gestures and pantomimes are not. Husserl's reasons [1] for not treating gestures and pantomimes as expressions in the same sense in which speech and parts of speech are so, are the following.

In the first place, gestures etc. are *not* felt by the person who produces them as being phenomenally identical (*phänomenal eins*) with, i.e. as being indistinguishable from, the experiences sought to be expressed through them. Speech, however, as an expression is felt to be indistinguishable from that which is expressed through it: genuine expressions, it may be said, are not felt to be other than what is expressed through them. Secondly, gestures etc. function as signs, or as marks, of the mental states of one who produces them, but *by themselves* – unless suitably interpreted by the hearer – they do not 'say' anything.

After having distinguished expressions from other signs and the function of meaning from the function of signifying (pointing to, or marking out), Husserl proceeds to insist that expressions nevertheless function as signs. They do so, according to Husserl,

[1] *L.U.*, II, 1, p. 30–31.

in what he calls communicative speech.[1] In communicative speech, expressions serve the hearer as *signs* for the thoughts of the speaker, for the latter's beliefs, doubts, wishes, and also for his pleasures and pains. Husserl calls this function of expressions the 'pronouncing-function.' Certain psychical experiences of the speaker are 'pronounced' through expressions in communicative speech. In a wider sense of the term, all those mental experiences which the hearer attributes to the speaker are 'pronounced'; in a narrower sense only those mental acts are 'pronounced' that *confer meaning* upon the expression concerned. A perceptual statement 'this table is brown' announces, in one sense of the term 'announcement', the speaker's perceptual experience and, in a narrower sense of the same term, his act of judging or believing. On hearing a person uttering such a statement, the hearer comes to know, on the one hand, that the speaker is having a certain perceptual experience and, on the other, that he is making an assertion that... or entertaining a belief that... The hearer apprehends the speaker as a person who is believing, doubting, desiring, questioning etc.

With regard to this 'pronouncing-function,' a distinction no doubt must be drawn between predicative statements and statements expressing the speaker's wish, desire, decisions, questions etc. In the case of a predicative statement the hearer no doubt apprehends the speaker as one who is making an assertion or expressing a belief, and it is only in this sense that the speaker's acts of asserting and believing are thereby 'pronounced.' But it would be wrong if one describes this fact by saying that in the case of a predicative statement the speaker's mental experiences like believing or asserting are objectively (*gegenständlich*) apprehended by the hearer. In the case of perceptual statements, what is objectively apprehended by the hearer is not that the speaker is having a perceptual experience but merely the state of affairs, the *Sachverhalt*, referred to. In cases of predicative statements, we could say, the 'pronounced' and the 'objectively apprehended' fall apart: the former being certain mental experiences of the speaker, and the latter being the *Sachverhalt*, the state of affairs referred to (e.g. that S is P). In case of statements expressing questions, orders, decisions,

[1] *ibid.*, p. 32.

desires etc., what are 'pronounced' are the speaker's questioning, ordering, deciding, desiring etc., and it is precisely these that are also 'objectively apprehended.' [1]

4.2.　In this connection, several remarks should be made at once. Husserl takes communication to be the original function of language.[2] He does not however sufficiently warn us against confusing the distinction between the function of 'pronouncing' and the function of 'being a mark of.' In fact, he himself is not free from confusion. While discussing the function of 'pronouncing' for example, he speaks of expressions as marks of the thoughts or other mental experiences of the speaker.[3] It is necessary to emphasize that even in its 'pronouncing' function speech never becomes so degenerate as to become a mere mark. A mark never makes us *see*, or even apprehend, the signified; at its best, the presence of the mark makes us believe in the presence of the signified. But the expressions make the hearer see, or even apprehend the speaker as having certain mental experiences: expressions therefore are not just marks of the experiences, but announce them and reveal them to the other.

Further, it would be an error to suppose that in communicative speech the *only* function fulfilled by expressions is that of 'pronouncement.' If that were so, communicative speech could only convey to the hearer reports about the mental experiences of the speaker, which certainly is not the case. The meaning-function is also operative and remains predominant (even in communicative speech) in the case of predicative statements.

Lastly, saying that expressions 'pronounce' certain mental experiences of the speaker is not the same as saying that the expressions *name* those mental experiences: 'pronouncing' and 'naming' are not the same. Husserl would rather contend that expressions are of two kinds: those which name and pronounce the same content, and those in whose case the named and the pronounced contents are different. Statements expressing

---

[1] This seems to be Husserl's view at the end of the 6th Investigation in § 70 of *L.U.*, II, 2. In *L.U.*, II, 1, Ch. 1, § 7, however, Husserl seems to be holding a slightly different opinion inasmuch as he says that sentences expressing desire also 'pronounce' a *judgment* about the desire. See § 16 of this work for further discussions of this issue.

[2] *L.U.*, II, 1, p. 32.

[3] *ibid.*, p. 33.

questions, desires, orders, etc. both pronounce *and* name the
mental states of questioning, desire, order etc. In the case of
predicative statements, as has already been pointed out, the
named and the pronounced are quite different: what is pronounced is a belief, what is named is a *Sachverhalt*. This distinction between the two groups of expressions could be stated
in another way. In the case of the expressions of the first group,
the corresponding modified expressions formed by prefixing 'I
request...', 'I ask...' or 'I order...' are not new expressions
but belong to the original unmodified expressions; in the case
of the expressions of the second group the original unmodified
expressions and the corresponding modified expressions are not
equivalent. The statement 'I believe that S is P' might be false;
it is false if I am not really believing that S is P, if I am in fact
not free from doubt regarding the *Sachverhalt*. But the statement
'S is P' might still be true, which only shows that the two statements are not equivalent.

In another sense of the term 'pronouncement,' the pronounced
and the named contents might fall apart even in the case of the
expressions of the first group. In this sense, what is pronounced
by an expression of the sort 'I want a glass of water' is *the
judgment* that I have such and such desire, and not the desire
itself, the latter being the content named: the pronounced and
the named therefore are still different.

It might be safer to say that Husserl recognises only one class
of expressions in whose case the pronounced and the named
contents unmistakably coincide. These are the so-called 'occasional' expressions (Husserl) or 'indexical' expressions (Peirce),
or 'ego-centric' particulars (Russell). These expressions, Husserl
tells us, have *"auf den augenblicklichen Inhalt der Kundgebung
eine nennende Beziehung"*: they *name* the momentary content
pronounced by them.[1]

4.3.   After having distinguished genuine expressions from
marks, we found Husserl telling us that expressions nevertheless functioned in communicative speech as marks of the
psychic states of the speaker. We remarked that although expressions exercised a pronouncing function in so far as they

[1] *ibid.*, p. 79.

made the hearer *apprehend* the mental experiences of the speaker, yet this function of pronouncing was not exactly the same as that of being a mark of something. Expressions, we said, never become so degenerate as to function as mere marks. There is however one group of expressions that seem to falsify our contention, for are not proper names mere unmeaning marks as Mill has contended?

Even with regard to proper names, Husserl sticks to his distinction between expressions and marks.[1] Like all expressions proper names also function as marks in so far as they pronounce to the hearer the *representations* belonging to the speaker's mind. But the proper name primarily refers not to the representation (of the object named), but to the represented *object*. (Mill, when he treats a proper name as a mark, connects it with the representation which the name awakens in us.) In its relation to the *object* represented, as distinct from the representation evoked, the proper name is not a mere mark but a genuine expression. The mark, Husserl goes on to tell us, is necessarily mark of an existent something; the named however need not exist. The proper name therefore is not a mere mark. The distinction between connotative and non-connotative terms is *not* the distinction between the meaningful and the unmeaning. Both the connotative and the non-connotative terms of Mill are meaningful signs, and hence expressions. Similarly, Mill's distinction between what a name denotes and what a name connotes is not the distinction between what a name names and what it *means*. These distinctions were left unclarified by Mill.

§ 5. Husserl has said that expressions were originally meant for the purpose of communicating. In communicative speech, expressions exercise the function of pronouncement in addition to their meaning-function. (But we have emphasized that even in communicative speech it is the meaning-function that predominates in the case of predicative statements.) Are the two functions, the meaning – and the pronouncing-functions, inseparable? Or, is it possible to find the one even in the absence of the other? Husserl's answer seems to be that although it is possible to find the meaning-function in the absence of the

[1] *ibid.*, pp. 57 ff.

pronouncing-function, it is not possible to find the pronouncing-function in the absence of the meaning-function. The impossibility of finding an expression that merely pronounces but does not also mean is due to the fact, that expressions are defined as meaningful signs, whereby the meaning-function may be regarded as belonging to expressions qua expressions. Even in the case of non-predicative statements, this function is operative. Only, the meant and the pronounced contents may coincide, as in the case of statements expressing desire, order, etc. For cases where the pronouncing function is entirely absent, Husserl directs us to the use of expressions in non-communicative speech, that is to say in monologues, *"im einsamen Seelenleben."* [1] Here expressions retain their meanings, indeed the same meanings which they have in communicative speech. But in monologues they do not announce anything; they do not any longer function as marks of mental experiences. It would not do to say that even if there is no hearer to whom the announcement is made, it is yet possible that the words serve the speaker himself as marks of his own mental experiences. Husserl's reason for rejecting this suggestion is hardly satisfactory. He argues that a mark functions as a mark only by being itself an existent something, whereas in lonely thought one operates not with actually existent expressions but with mere representations – phantasized or imagined – of them. Since our thought is not disturbed by the non-existence of the words, the expressions concerned do not function as marks. This argument is not convincing, for the mere representation of a mark (say, of a danger signal) could under circumstances act as a warning. I should think Husserl could have, with more persuasive effect, relied upon another argument (which has been stated above and of which he makes use in a different context): he could have pointed out that whereas a mark and that of which it is a mark are felt to be different, the speaker does not feel the expression – actual or imagined – to be other than that which is expressed through them. Besides, what a predicative statement announces – in communicative speech – is the speaker's act of believing, or the fact that the speaker believes in such-and-such fact; and yet it is clear that to the speaker himself, in the loneliness of his mind, the expression

[1] *ibid.*, p. 35.

'S is P' does not announce his own act of believing, for his consciousness of his own believing is an immediately felt, pre-
verbal awareness, not in need of being announced. For him,
the expression, or its representation, simply *means*. Here,
according to Husserl, we have the essential nature of expressions qua expressions, i.e. in their unadulterated meaning-
function.

5.1.   It is necessary and important for our purpose to thrash
out the relevance of Husserl's contrast between communicative
speech and speech in the loneliness of one's mental life. Husserl makes much of this distinction and utilises it chiefly for the purpose of
separating the pronouncing function from the meaning function.
This helps him further to show that the essence of an expression
qua expression lies not in its pronouncing function, that is to
say, not in its use as a mark but in the meaning function. The
contrast under consideration also shows, according to Husserl,
that the *real* existence of the expression as a physical event is
not essential to the expression as an expression, so that even the
mere representation – imagined or fancied – of the expression
would equally well fulfil the essential meaning function.

The contrast however is misleading and is liable to divert
our attention from one of the important criteria which a satisfactory theory of meaning has to fulfil. For if the contrast is the
same as that between public thinking and private thinking,[1]
then Husserl would seem to be defending the view that it is in
private thinking that one catches hold of the meaning function
in its purity. This however should justify any attempt to base
one's theory of meaning on the so-called private thinking. And
yet one could very well argue that such emphasis on private
thinking is likely to yield ruinous consequences. Price has pointed
out that what is called the Image theory of thinking starts from
private thinking. The risk that we run is psychologism and the
consequent relativism. The true nature of thought, it might be
argued, manifests itself in reflection upon its communicative
function; for here in communicative speech, subjectivity is
overcome and thought exhibits itself as an objective, over-
individual process. Both the Hegelians and the operationalists

[1] H. H. Price, *loc. cit.*, pp. 184 ff.

recognize this: Hegelians, for they look upon thought as an over-individual process, and the operationalists, for in spite of their conventionalism they see that the rules determining the meaningfulness of symbolism are nevertheless objective. Husserl also, as is well known, recognizes the objectivity of meanings and has offered the most successful criticism of psychologism in recent times. It is in the fitness of things therefore that he should not have, quite contrary to his real intentions, relied on the contrast between private and public thinking in the manner he does.

§ 6.   It is now time to put together the various functions of expressions and to enquire into their precise nature and philosophical importance.

Husserl ascribes to expressions three basic functions: (1) the pronouncing function, (2) the meaning function, and (3) the naming function. Of these, it is (2) alone which makes expressions into expressions. Every expression pronounces some mental state or states of the speaker. Besides making such a pronouncement, every expression also conveys a meaning. And it also refers to an object. Corresponding to the three functions, there are thus three senses in which one could speak of what is 'expressed' through an expression. What is expressed may be the pronounced mental state, or the meaning conveyed or the object referred to.

Husserl's three functions may be compared with Bühler's.[1] Bühler distinguishes between (1) the symptomatic function, (2) the signal function, and (3) the descriptive function. An expression serves as a symptom of some mental state of the speaker; at the same time it works as a signal for the hearer to behave in an appropriate manner. But the expression is also *about* something, and so far it describes a situation. Of these three functions, it is only (3) that is philosophically relevant. (1) and (2) are amenable to a causal-physicalistic theory of language. But such a physicalistic theory is bound to miss the unique character of the descriptive function of language.[2] Bühler's 'symptomatic' function is the same as Husserl's 'pronouncing' function. The

---

[1] K. Bühler, *Sprachtheorie*, 1934, pp. 25–28.
[2] K. Popper, "Language and the Body-Mind Problem," *Proceedings of the XIth International Congress of Philosophy*, Vol. VII, pp. 101–107.

'signal' function is not recognized by Husserl, but it could be said in justification of Husserl's omission that this 'signal' function is not what imparts meaning to an expression, that is to say, is not what makes an expression into an expression and is so far irrelevant. Bühler's 'descriptive function,' on the other hand, includes Husserl's other two functions: the meaning- and the naming-functions.

6.1.   The pronouncing function having been referred to in an earlier section, we turn now to the other two functions and to the corresponding contents. The distinction between meaning and naming (or referring) calls for immediate comparison with Frege's similar and more well-known distinction. The necessity of distinguishing between meaning and reference would become clear if we would convince ourselves (i) that expressions with the same meaning may have different references, and (ii) that expressions with the same reference may have different meanings. There are besides two more possibilities: (iii) expressions may differ both in meaning and in reference. Lastly, (iv) they may agree in both.

For examples of (i), consider the two sentences 'Bucephalus is a horse' and 'Mayflower is a horse.' The meaning of the expression 'a horse' remains unchanged in the two cases, but the reference is different in each case.

For examples of (ii), consider the two expressions 'The conqueror of Jena' and 'The vanquished of Waterloo.' They have the same reference, but different meanings. The same holds good of the pair of expressions: 'the equilateral triangle' and 'the equiangular triangle.'

For examples of (iii), consider the two expressions 'man' and 'table': they differ in their references as well as in their meanings.

It is at once obvious that the distinction runs closely parallel to Frege's, though the terminological departure must be noted: Frege's *Sinn* = Husserl's *Bedeutung*, while Frege's *Bedeutung* = Husserl's *Gegenstand* (the named or the referred).

6.2.   Postponing to the next chapter a consideration of what Husserl means by 'meaning' (*Bedeutung* or *Sinn*), let us try to understand here what he means by the '*Gegenstand*,' the object of naming or reference, of an expression.

Every expression is *about* something, *über Etwas*.[1] It not only has a meaning, but relates itself to an object. This relation however between an expression and its object is not always one of naming. Not all expressions name their objects. Husserl writes, the object is *"genannt oder sonstwie bezeichnet."* The modern terminology of 'referring' would perhaps be more appropriate in this context. An expression refers to an object; 'naming' would then be a specific kind of referring. It is not very clear how Husserl would characterize this specific kind of referring called 'naming.' At one place at least [2] he says that only those expressions that are capable of functioning as complete subjects of predicative statements are names. In accordance with this restriction, the mere noun does *not* amount to a name. In order to be a name, it must enter into certain syntactical relationships and must be preceded by the definite or indefinite article.[3] 'Horse' is not a name, but 'the horse' is a name. *Expressions other than names also refer*, that is to say, are about some object.

One point where Husserl differs from Frege concerns the reference of sentences: whereas according to Frege, the meaning (*Sinn*) of a sentence is the thought (*Gedanke*) expressed and its reference (*Bedeutung*) is the truth-value (*Wahrheitswert*),[4] for Husserl a sentence means a *Gedanke* but *refers* to a *Sachlage* or state of affairs.[5] Consider the two propositions 'a is greater than b' and 'b is smaller than a.' They refer to the same state of affairs, but they differ in their meanings that is to say in the *gedanklich* ways they refer to it.

Thus the reference of an expression is partly determined by its meaning. In the first place, an expression refers only in so far as it also means. But, secondly, we could also say that an expression refers *through* its meaning. Where meanings differ there the modes of reference also should differ, though the

---

[1] *L.U.*, II, 1, p. 46.
[2] *ibid.*, p. 463.
[3] Compare G. Ryle: "Incidentally it is not true even that all ordinary general nouns can function by themselves as subjects of sentences ..." (in *British Philosophy in Mid-century*, ed. by Mace, p. 250).
[4] G. Frege, "Über Sinn und Bedeutung," *Zeitschrift für Philosophie und philosophische Kritik*, NF 100, 1892, pp. 32–34.
[5] *L.U.*, II, 1, p. 48.

object referred to may be the same; such expressions refer to
the same object, though in different ways.

The other factor which determines the reference of an expression is its use. An expression now refers to this object, now
to that, and this shifting character of its reference is determined
by its use.[1] So far then Husserl would be in agreement with
Strawson's distinction between an expression and its use.[2] But
the really decisive question in this connection is, whether Husserl
would agree with Strawson in holding that while meaning is a
function of expressions and sentences, referring is a function of
their use. At least at one place Husserl would seem to be saying
what is very much like Strawson's: *"Also einen Ausdruck mit
Sinn gebrauchen und sich ausdrückend auf den Gegenstand be-
ziehen (den Gegenstand vorstellen) ist einerlei."* [3] To *use* an expression meaningfully and to make it refer to an object amount
to the same. If this were so, reference would be, also according
to Husserl, the function of the *use* of an expression and not of
the mere expression. But since Husserl also attributes the referring function to expressions as such, his opinion on this
matter would perhaps be something like this: though an expression in itself has a reference, this reference remains indefinite
so long as we do not consider a specific use of it. Apart from its
use, an expression is not without reference; only, its reference is
vague and further determinable. It is its use that gives it the
required determination. Husserl would not further agree with the
Frege-Wittgensteinian view that a name stands for something only
in the context of a sentence.[4] A name as such has the logical function
of naming and this is prior to all predicative thought.[5] The distinction between naming and judging cannot be in any case overlooked.[6]

6.3.   Modern philosophers have discussed what has come to
be called *this paradox of reference*, and it is time to ask how Husserl would solve these paradoxes. The problem that gives rise
to the paradox is: how can sentences like 'The present king of

---

[1] *L.U.*, II, 1, p. 49.
[2] P. F. Strawson, "On Referring," *Mind*, 1950.
[3] *L.U.*, II, 1, p. 54.
[4] cp. L. Wittgenstein, *Tractatus Logico-Philosophicus*, 3.3.
[5] cp. P. T. Geach, "Subject and Predicate," *Mind*, 1950.
[6] *L.U.*, II, 1, pp. 466–471.

France is wise' be significant even when there is nothing to which 'The present king of France' refers. And yet since such sentences do make sense there must be some fictitious entity called 'The present king of France.'

The classic solution of this problem is offered by Russell, and the almost classic answer to Russell by Strawson. Russell's solution consists in arguing that the phrase 'The present king of France' is not, despite its appearance to the contrary, a name at all but a description. For the relevant distinction between a name and a description in the present context, let me quote from Russell:

"if "a" be a name, it *must* name something: what does not name anything is not a name, and therefore, if intended to be a name, is a symbol devoid of meaning, whereas a description, like 'The present king of France,' does not become incapable of occurring significantly merely on the ground that it describes nothing...." [1]

Whereas a logically proper name is meaningless if there is nothing that it names, a description has its meaning independently of the question whether there is anything which satisfies the description or not.

Russell's theory is based on two conceptions: first, that of a logically proper name and secondly, that of the logical subject of a proposition. A logically proper name is a name that designates an object with which we are immediately acquainted. From this it would follow that the designatum of a name must exist, that a proposition in which a name occurs as a name is *about* the designatum of the name, and that, in this sense, the designatum is a constituent of the proposition in which its name occurs.

Secondly, if a subject-predicate proposition is to be significant, then there must *be* something, referred to by the *logical* subject. Where this is not the case, i.e., where a subject-predicate proposition is significant without the subject being a logically proper name and without there being something referred to, Russell would suggest (i) that the grammatical form of the proposition misleads us as to the logical form, and (ii) that the proposition should be further analysed.

[1] B. Russell, *Introduction to Mathematical Philosophy*, London, 1919, p. 179.

Strawson's reply to the above is as follows: – while meaning is a function of the sentence or expression, mentioning or referring and truth or falsity are functions of the *use* of the sentence or expression. The meaning of an expression cannot be identified with the object it is used to refer to on a particular occasion. Russell, according to Strawson, committed the error of confusing meaning with referring; since the sentence had meaning, Russell argued, it must be about something that *is*, and hence arose the problem which he tried to solve by his theory of description. The sentence 'The present King of France is wise' is in any case meaningful; only, its *use* by any one now would be a spurious use whereas it could have been genuinely used by any one living, let us say, in the 17th century.

We are to find out where Husserl stands with regard to this problem. It is at once obvious that Husserl would reject Russell's conception of logically proper names. He would treat all expressions capable of functioning as complete subjects of predicative statements as names.[1] 'The present King of France' would be according to him a name. How then would he resolve the paradox that the statement 'The present King of France is wise' could be significant without yet being about anything to which it refers? There is no doubt that Husserl would fall back, as Strawson does, on the distinction between meaning and reference and would argue that the meaningfulness of an expression (or of a sentence) does not depend upon its referring function and that the meaning function being prior to the referring function would be rather presupposed by the latter. An expression, he would agree, may be used to refer now to this object, now to that even though its meaning remains unaffected by these vicissitudes of its referring function. The object referred to may be fictitious, but that does not make the expression meaningless.[2] A Russellian of course may retort by pointing out that this way of putting the thing commits us to admit Meinongian fictitious entities. How can we at all speak of a fictitious *entity*? Strawson *might* reply that since expressions as such do not refer and since it is only by *genuinely using* them that we refer, any one uttering the sentence 'The King of France is wise' in our times is making a

---

[1] See § 18 in Ch. V of this book for Husserl's Theory of Names.
[2] *L.U.*, II, 1, pp. 54–55.

spurious use of it and hence is *not referring at all*. There is then no need of postulating fictitious entities. When making such a pseudo-use of the sentence, one is not talking about anything at all; but that does not take away the significance either of the expression or of the sentence.

Since, as we have maintained, according to Husserl expressions qua expressions (and not merely uses of them) refer, he cannot possibly go the whole way in Strawson's company. We have seen how far the two would agree: their agreement consists in making the significance of an expression immune from the changing fortunes of its reference. But, holding as he does that an expression as such refers, he cannot dismiss any use of 'The present King of France is wise' as spurious *in the sense of* not referring at all. On the other hand, if he does take it as referring (and if he is not willing to agree with Russell that 'The present King of France' is not a name but a description and that the sentence requires further analysis), how can he avoid committing himself to the postulation of the dreaded Meinongian entities?

Let us pause a while to examine how far Strawson's analysis really takes us. Strawson's solution consists in maintaining three propositions: (i) that an expression as such does not refer; (ii) that only a genuine use of an expression refers; and (iii) that where we are using an expression but are not referring, we are making a pseudo-use of it. Now, it is (iii) which makes us suspicious. How do you know that a certain use of an expression does not refer? 'Because the use is a spurious one,' would be the answer. But how do you know that it is a spurious use? 'Because it does not refer at all'! The circularity involved in the argument is immediately clear. The source of this circularity is Strawson's refusal to attribute reference to certain uses; this refusal is then sought to be justified by calling these uses 'spurious,' as distinguished from those uses that refer and are therefore genuine.

'How could you deny that certain uses of expressions do not refer at all,?' I may be asked at this point. 'Is it not obvious that any one who now utters the sentence 'The present King of France is wise,' is not referring at all? And, therefore, is it not equally obvious that he is making a spurious use of the expression?'

Husserl would agree that the use under consideration does not refer to an existent; but it is not for that reason wholly free from reference. 'Does not that invite the Meinongian ghosts?', would be the rejoinder. Certainly not, we reply. (Let us not forget that the Meinongian ghosts are less injurious than the dread they have aroused in philosophers.) The Meinongian ghosts, the Russellian dissection of them and the Strawsonian escape are all conditioned by a *too ready interest* in *ontology*, in what is or exists (and in what subsists). If only we suppress for the moment our interest in ontology and look at the phenomenon itself, we shall find that the use under consideration refers, but the reference remains a *merely intended reference*, that is to say – borrowing Husserl's pet terminology – its intention is incapable of being fulfilled. One may even distinguish between two different ways in which the sentence 'The present King of France is wise' may be used by any one uttering it now. If the person uttering it is utterly ignorant of the political situation of contemporary France, his use of it would be different from the use of one who (like Russell and Strawson) utters it even with the knowledge that France has no monarchy at present. In the former case, there would not only be a referring, there would also be an intention directed towards its own fulfilment (though the intention is doomed to be frustrated); in the latter case, there is a mere reference accompanied by the sure conviction that the reference intended would never be fulfilled. Call it a spurious use, if you so like. The use is spurious not because it does not refer but because the intended reference either may be subsequently found to be *incapable of* fulfilment or is already known to be so.

The same principle would apply to cases like 'Pegasus' or 'round-square.' They are names, but "*der genannte Gegenstand ja gar nicht als existierender zu gelten braucht.*" [1] What is the harm in speaking of 'fictitious objects,' if only we know that we are not hypostatizing them! There is far lesser reason for apprehension if we are *not* ontologising.

---

[1] *L.U.*, II, 1, 59. Husserl later on distinguishes between names that posit the existence of an entity and names that do not. Compare *ibid.*, pp. 462 f.

CHAPTER III

THINKING AND MEANING

§ 7.   The essence of an expression lies in its meaning function. Husserl devotes a large part of his logical studies to an analysis of this function of expressions. He started with the distinction between meaning and reference. If therefore in his theory of meaning he leans towards Platonism, such Platonism cannot be traced to "an earlier failure to appreciate that meaning and naming are distinct." [1] Since our main task is a correct appreciation of the nature of thought, it is the problem of meaning which shall interest us most. The discussions on reference *were only of subsidiary* relevance.

Reference has been made earlier to the Image theory of thinking. In our exposition of Husserl's theory of meaning, we would again go back to it and prefix the exposition with a few more remarks on some questions intimately connected with it. Let us get back to Berkeley's arguments against the Lockean (or what has been supposed to be the Lockean) doctrine of abstract ideas. There is no doubt that this notion of abstract idea – the idea, e.g., of triangle-in-general – forms the core of the classical account of thinking, just as there is no denying the fact that the Berkeleyan argument has inspired a series of attempts to expose that classical account. "What is more easy than for anyone to look a little into his own thoughts, and there try whether he has, or can attain to have, an idea that shall correspond with the description that is here given of the general idea of a triangle, which is *neither oblique, nor rectangled, equilateral, equicrural, nor scalene, but all and none of these at once?'* [2]

---

[1] W. V. O. Quine, "Semantics and Abstract Objects," *Proceedings of the American Academy of Arts and Sciences*, Vol. 80, No. 1, p. 91.

[2] Berkeley, *Principles of Human Knowledge* (Introduction, para 13), quoted by G. J. Warnock in his *Berkeley*, 1953, p. 67.

The merit and also the fault of Berkeley's argument are immediately clear. Berkeley has successfully exposed the absurdity of abstract images. The real fault of his argument does not lie in the fact that he exaggerates the definiteness of our imagery. Warnock has rightly pointed out that Berkeley survives such criticism.[1] The real fault lies in Berkeley's imagist notion of thinking. Locke's abstract idea was understood as an abstract image, and it is no wonder that Berkeley's blow should prove fatal. The abstract image dwindled. But the victory was poor, for the enemy had put up only a poor defence. General idea and general image are not the same. Locke did not distinguish between idea in the sense of image and idea in the sense of meaning.[2]

Locke takes his start from the indisputable contention that every general term has its meaning. From this quite acceptable premise he proceeds however to the very different conclusion that this meaning is a general image formed by *separating* the varying features of the particulars to whom the general name is applicable and by grouping together the features common to them. It is by such a *process of abstraction* that we arrive at the abstract idea of triangle in general that is neither isosceles nor equilateral nor scalene.

7.1.   Rightly therefore Husserl enquires into the nature of this process called abstraction by which we reach the level of abstract thinking. In their theories of abstraction, the empiricists Locke, Berkeley, Mill and Hume share in a common error. Their difference is only one of emphasis.

Locke believed in mind's ability to bring about a real separation of the components in the representation of a concrete object; some of these factors are grouped together so as to constitute an abstract image.

Mill, according to Husserl,[3] does not go as far as Locke. He rightly sees that a real separation is not possible though we can fix our exclusive attention on some of the attributes of a concrete object, disregarding the other attributes with which they are

[1] G. J. Warnock, *Berkeley*, pp. 67–69.
[2] *L.U.*, II, 1, pp. 128–9.
[3] *L.U.*, II, 1, pp. 137–8.

combined. Mill recognizes however that attention is never as completely exclusive as this. In the strict sense therefore we have no general ideas. But he also assures us that through "concentrative effort," we may succeed in making our attention exclusive to a large degree. Exclusive attention does not bring about real separation, but makes it possible "exactly *as if* we were able to conceive them separately from the rest." [1] This, of course, is made possible by the use of the name.

While Locke believed in real separation of the attributes, and Mill believed in exclusive attention, Berkeley takes up a more cautious position. Berkeley, it is well known, rejects, not general ideas as such, but only the so-called abstract general ideas. In other words, he does not believe in the real existence – mental or non-mental – of general ideas, of ideas that do not possess any of the differentiating characters belonging to the concrete particulars that exemplify them. But he did believe that it was possible to abstract only in the sense in which one could, for example, *consider* a given figure merely as a triangle without attending to the special properties of its sides or angles. Though in itself particular, an idea may be *used* [2] in such a way as to *become* general. Generality is a function of the *use* of a sign, not of the sign itself. The sign is used to stand – not for Locke's abstract idea – but for other particulars. Warnock does not see that Berkeley's notion of *use* in this context is not independent of the psychological doctrine of attention which vitiates the concept of abstraction in all three: Locke, Berkeley and Mill. Hume continues the psychological-genetic account of thinking of his predecessors. How does one particular *come to stand for* other particulars? Hume tries to solve this question by his theory of the association of ideas.

Against all such theories of abstraction – and the consequent accounts of thinking – Husserl offers the following objections:

(1) A psychological and genetic explanation of thinking must be kept apart from a logical clarification of the contents of such consciousness. The empirical theories of abstraction describe the process of abstraction in the language of cause and effect. They

---

[1] J. S. Mill, *An examination of Sir W. Hamilton's Philosophy*, 3rd edn., London, 1867, p. 377. Quoted by Husserl.
[2] cp. G. J. Warnock, *loc. cit.*, pp. 69–71.

miss thereby the unmistakably peculiar nature of that consciousness as well as of the contents of that consciousness.[1]

(2) The act of attending is not a descriptive constituent of our consciousness of generality. We *intend or mean* a generality. While installed in that mode of consciousness, we are not attending to anything in the sense in which the theory says we do.[2]

(3) The constituent attribute (e.g. triangularity, redness etc.) that is on this theory attended to is as much an individual as the concrete totality (e.g. a given triangle, a red object etc.) whose component it is. The act of attending to a concrete whole (this red tomato before me) and the act of attending to a part of that whole (e.g. its red colour) are of the same *sort*.[3] We do not thereby come to any new mode of consciousness or to any content that would be totally new. What we intend or mean when aware of a generality is neither a concrete perceptual object nor a part of the content of that object, but an Idea (the precise sense of which remains to be made clear).

(4) According to Berkeley and the nominalists following Berkeley, generality lies in the representative function of an image or of a name. Against this doctrine Husserl advances the following arguments:

(*a*) It is one thing to say that a sign – a name or an image – represents or suggests *each* one of the other particulars *taken separately*. It is quite another thing to say that the sign represents or suggests or means *all* As or *any* A. In the latter case, to say that the sign *stands for* something is wrong. For in this case the so-called sign (according to Husserl the expression, strictly speaking, is not a mere sign) is not *suggesting* this or that particular A, but, as it were, makes possible the consciousness of *all* As "*in einem einheitlichen Pulse, in einem homogenen und eigenartigen Akte.*"[4] This act intending *all* A or *any* A certainly relates itself to each particular A, but only indirectly and by implication.

(*b*) There is certainly a sense in which an individual image or a name does fulfil a representative function.[5] This is so in so far as the image or the name, the spoken or the written word,

[1] *L.U.*, II, 1, pp. 120, 144–6.
[2] *ibid.*, pp. 120, 146.
[3] *ibid.*, pp. 155–6.
[4] *ibid.*, p. 179.
[5] *ibid.*, pp. 174–5.

makes possible the *higher* intentional act of *meaning* a generality. The sensuous awareness of the image or the word serves as the starting point, the spring-board for the higher activity of thinking. But the two modes of awareness are distinct; so also are their objects.

(*c*) Applied to geometrical proofs, the above remark amounts to this: what happens in geometrical proofs is *not* – as Berkeley would have it – that we prove a property of a particular triangle ABC and only then subsequently use this particular triangle to stand for or represent all other particular triangles. We rather start by saying that ABC is *any* triangle. The image of the triangle drawn on the board or visualised serves as the mere spring-board for the thought of the *species* triangle, the proof being *from the very beginning* concerned with this universal idea.[1]

7.2.   At this point in our exposition, it would be proper to give a summary account of Husserl's principal arguments against nominalism.

We may say that according to Husserl the essence of nominalism as well as the principal source of its failure is *not* that it rejects universal entities, but that it overlooks that peculiar mode of consciousness which announces itself on the one hand in the living grasp of the sense of signs, in the actual understanding of them, in the intelligent meaning of expressions; and, on the other, in those correlative acts of fulfilment that constitute the genuine representation of the universal, in other words, "in that insightful process of ideation in which the universal itself is given." [2] For the nominalist, there is no *radical* difference between sensing and thinking, between sensuous apprehension of a particular i.e. the 'this-here,' and thought of a generality. It is precisely on this distinction – formulated as a radical difference – that Husserl's case rests. The ultimate appeal is to the *Bewusstseinsweise, die Weise der Intention*, to the new character of meaningful thought that rises as a superstructure upon the sensuous basis.[3]

Bearing this principal argument in mind, we might try to

---

[1] *ibid.*, pp. 180–1.
[2] *ibid.*, p. 145.
[3] *ibid.*, p. 187.

understand the case *for* nominalism, as formulated by Husserl.

At one place, Husserl distinguishes between three *forms* of generality: *an* A, *all* A, *the* A-in-general.[1] Their roles in thinking are illustrated in the sentences: 'ABC is a triangle', 'All triangles have their three angles equal to two right angles,' 'The triangle is a kind of plane figure.' The distinctions between these three forms of generality are then brought out in the following way:

The generality of *an A* belongs to the logical function of the predicate. The logical word '*an*' here expresses an irreducibly primitive logical form. Its very indeterminateness indicates its generality, but only the generality of the predicate. The generality consists in the 'logical possibility of propositions of a certain kind', or in the logical possibility of the same predicate's functioning in different propositions.[2]

The *all A* points to another primitive form of generality. What we mean, of course, relates itself to each and every member of the extent or denotation of A; but we do not mean each and every A separately, nor do we mean a collection, or even a possible totality of them. The idea of *all* is not a complex of singular representations, but has a unitary and unanalysable form.

The A again presents quite another form of generality, the generality of the *specific* meaning-content. This form lies closer to *all A*, but is nevertheless distinct from it: their difference is not verbal, not merely grammatical, but logical [3] and is reflected in the different modes of consciousness through which they are thought or represented.

After having distinguished between the three forms of generality, Husserl goes on to ask if these forms are not reducible to one another and if the *species A* ('the A') does not lie concealed in all three forms. The first question is answered in the negative. As to the second, Husserl concedes that even if the species A lies concealed, it is so only potentially. What he possibly means by this is that though the two other forms may be translated to the last one, yet the *species as such is not all that was meant* in the original forms.

---

[1] *ibid.*, p. 147.
[2] *ibid.*, p. 148.
[3] *ibid.*, p. 149.

Of these three different forms, the nominalist sees only the predicative and would, at most, seek to *reduce* the other two to the predicative generality. Now once this reduction is taken to be permissible it would further seem plausible that the predicative generality itself is reducible to resemblance relations. Instead of saying 'S is an A' and 'M is an A,' the nominalist would prefer saying 'S and M resemble in respect of....' [1] The nominalist is thereby committing two errors: in the first place, he misses the peculiarity of the other two forms of generality; and secondly, he distorts the nature even of that one form, i.e. the predicative, which he chooses and to which he seeks to reduce the other two.

§ 8. So much about nominalism for the present. Having distinguished between expressions and marks, we could now say that the *question of meaning concerns expressions* considered not as physical events but *as such*. This latter distinction should be made fundamental to any theory of meaning. Lewis for example recognizes that to confuse between an instance of an expression and the expression as such is an unprecise mode of speech.[2] The need for such a distinction has often been felt. Semanticists have distinguished between token-word and type-word: but their wellknown distinction does *not* go beyond the conception of expressions as physical events. In that case, the conception of a *type* can only be that of a recognizable physical pattern. But unless one is prepared to abandon the purely physicalistic conception of expressions, one must be willing to face the logical consequences of such a conception to refuse, like Goodman, to speak even of the letter 'A.' One cannot even consistently speak of an A-inscription. [3]

An expression *qua* expression is therefore more than a merely physical event. According to Lewis, a linguistic expression is constituted by the association of a verbal symbol and a fixed meaning.[4] According to Husserl, an expression as such is constituted by a unity of the physical aspect and the meaning aspect: *"Der Wortlaut ist zunächst eins mit der Bedeutungs-intention."* [5]

[1] B. Russell, *Logic and Knowledge*, London, 1956, p. 206.
[2] L. Linsky (ed.), *Semantics and the Philosophy of Language*, Illinois, 1952, p. 51.
[3] N. Goodman, *The Structure of Appearance*, Harvard, 1951, especially pp. 287 ff.
[4] L. Linsky, *loc. cit.*, p. 51.
[5] *L.U.*, II, 1, p. 38.

If an expression as such is constituted by its meaning and is not an expression without it, it follows that one cannot even strictly say that an expression 'expresses' its meaning.[1] To be an expression is to be animated by its entire meaning. An associationist explanation of this unity would be as inadequate as a mechanistic explanation of biological phenomena. [This analogy is here offered with a full consciousness of the fact that it is likely to stimulate the critics to warn us that we would thereby be thinking of meaning on the analogy of a soul or an entelechy inhabiting a physical framework, not unlike the 'ghost in the machine'. In anticipation of such a criticism, let me remind the intending critics that in the controversy between 'mechanism' and 'vitalism' there is a 'true' vitalism as distinguished from a 'false' vitalism, that the antimechanists have long since abandoned the entelechy-theory, that what they defend now is the autonomy of the biological sciences and no simple-minded myth of a 'ghost in the machine'.]

In his *Formale und Transzendentale Logik*, Husserl speaks of the *Idealität des Sprachlichen*.[2] A linguistic expression is not the passing physical phenomenon, but an ideal structure that is capable of 'being again'. It is easy to dismiss this as a piece of antiquated Platonism. It would be wiser however to pause and to enquire if there is any sense behind this Platonism. We do speak of the same expression as recurring. A word, a sentence, a theory, a geometrical proof are all capable of being repeated; the physical event, the written shape and the uttered sound are irrevocably unique. In what sense then could we speak of *the same* expression? Certainly not in the physicalistic sense! The sense in which an expression can *be again*, can retain its identity in discourse, can be revived, re-presented and re-understood is exactly the sense in which it is an ideal structure.

This ideality of a linguistic expression could be described, however, in two different levels. First, a linguistic expression is an entity that belongs to the *geistige Welt* or the *Kultur-welt*, and not, as we have emphasized above, to the physical nature. In this respect it bears comparison to a piece of music: Beethoven's Fifth Symphony is capable of being reproduced without losing

[1] *ibid.*, p. 39.
[2] *F.u.t.L.*, pp. 17–19.

its essential identity. Secondly, the ideality of an expression is also the ideality of its meaning: this precisely is the theme of our enquiry. It may however be noted here that these two aspects are inseparable and constitute an intimate unity that permits distinction but no division.

Let us direct our attention towards a printed word taken as a merely physical pattern.[1] Once we do this we have the usual mode of outer perception; but the object perceived is no more a word or a meaningful expression. But again as soon as it functions as a word or as an expression, the characteristic of its 'representation' undergoes a total change. The word still continues to be presented to us in outer perception. But we are not any longer interested in this aspect of it. Husserl would say that the intuitive representation in which the *physical* appearance of the word is constituted undergoes an essential modification. The physical pattern enters into a new *intentional unity*.

8.1.   Once we fix the nature of expressions in this way and thereby circumscribe the problem of meaning as pertaining to expressions only in *that* sense, we are on the way towards an understanding of Husserl's theory of meaning. For all forms of psychologism are thereby forthright excluded from the theory. The already discarded Image theory is a typical variety of psychologism. Two more points regarding this Image theory of meaning could be suggested here by way of a final rejection of that theory.

(i) First, so strong is the temptation to identify meaning with an image, a mental picture, or an inner experience, that even Bradley who started by clearly distinguishing between image and meaning ultimately succumbed to it; the meaning, he said, is a part of the content of an image abstracted from the psychical existence of the latter. Blanshard has rightly drawn attention to the absurdity of this compromise: "If the image is what Bradley says it is, a mere fact as opposed to meaning, 'a hard particular,' 'an event in my history,' how can a piece of it be eternal and a part of the physical world?" [2] The relation between

---

[1] *L.U.*, II, 1, pp. 40–41.
[2] B. Blanshard, *The Nature of Thought*, London, 1939, Vol. I, p. 448.

image and meaning, or, speaking generally, between any *'veri-ficatory' experience* and meaning must be formulated in an altogether different language. The relation is neither identity nor that of a whole to its part!

(ii) Many authors who reject the Image theory in the case of what is called abstract thinking (e.g. of mathematical or metaphysical thinking) nevertheless feel tempted to retain it, or some variety of it, in the case of what might be called 'perceptual judgments.' When looking at the wall before me I say 'this wall is white,' it is tempting to suggest that my *meaning* consists in the actual sensuous experience accompanying and making possible my judgment. If I am not actually seeing the white wall but am having a clear image of it in my mind when I utter the sentence, then – the theory would suggest – my meaning consists in the images occurring in my mind.

This restricted form of the Image theory shall fare no better. It fails to take notice of the undeniable fact that what is meant in such an assertion or in any 'perceptual judgment' – whether it is accompanied by an actual 'corresponding' sensuous experience or by a mere 'illustrating' image – is *not* any such experience or image but something objective, something that could be communicated to and shared by others. To say the least, one should agree with Stout [1] that the judgment 'This wall is white' refers not to the speaker's private experience at the moment but to a "permanent possibility" of experiences: so far at least, *though only so far*, some modern positivistic accounts of the situation are right (that is to say, in so far as these accounts take the meaning out of the inner experience of the speaker alone and make it consist in future *possible* experiences of others as well.)

Husserl's own discussion of the mental picture-theory is embodied in §§ 17–18 of the First Investigation in the *Logische Untersuchungen* Vol. 2, part I. For his rejection of this theory even in connection with the so-called perceptual judgments, we are to look into § 4 of the 6th Investigation in the same work Vol. 2 part 2. In this latter paragraph Husserl takes up a perceptual judgment and argues that the meaning of the judgment

---

[1] cfr. G. F. Stout, "Bradley's Theory of Judgment" included in his *Studies in Philosophy and Psychology*, London, 1930.

retains its identity in the midst of changing perceptions and also for different percipients. The perceptual basis could completely disappear without thereby the statement ceasing to be meaningful or even without its changing its meaning. Perhaps there is some image and that also so disconnected as to be a poor substitute for perception. In the end it is possible that the hearer understands my sentence without having any relevant imagery at all.

8.2. There is thus an appreciable measure of agreement between Husserl and Wittgenstein (of the *Philosophical Investigations*) so far as the rejection of the mental picture theory is concerned. And the agreement (which is an interesting theme for any student of contemporary philosophy) does not end here. There is in the *Philosophical Investigations* a near rejection of the very idea of a criterion of meaningfulness: a feature that brings that work nearer to the phenomenologist's camp.

The idea of a criterion of meaningfulness is recent in origin. But even within hardly three decades of its life history – leaving aside its historical affiliations to the 'old fathers' – this idea has undergone vicissitudes of fortune that are enough to justify its abandonment. Starting with an identification of meaning with 'method of verification,' the theory soon abandoned its emphasis on identification and came to look upon verification as a criterion of meaningfulness. This was followed by the distinction between verification in practice and verification in principle. A more appreciable compromise was made with the switch-over to the restricted view that if a statement is meaningful some sensible experiences must be *relevant* to determining its truth and falsity. Evans has rightly shown that the verification theory is a recommendatory definition of the terms 'tautologous' and 'empirical,' and that in no case could it be regarded as limiting the range of meaningful sentences.[1] Philosophy *cannot legislate* as to what should and what should not be treated as meaningful.

At this stage there is another likely move that should be avoided. The collapse of the idea of a criterion of meaningfulness combined with the realisation that what was paraded as an

[1] J. L. Evans, "On Meaning and Verification," *Mind*, 1953, pp. 1–14.

objectively binding criterion was really a concealed proposal
has led many to the almost tragic confession that philosophy
can *only* legislate, that is to say, put forward linguistic proposals,
in the present case as to what the most *desirable* use of the
predicate 'meaningful' is. It may be true that the so-called
criterion was a mere proposal, but philosophers can do no
better than making alternative recommendations.

Both Husserl and Wittgenstein would agree in rejecting this
conception of philosophy. "What we have rather to do is to
accept the everyday language-game... attempts at justification
need to be rejected." [1] (It should be noted that philosophy,
according to the move we are criticising, not merely recommends
– for that would make its task trifling – but should justify its
recommendations). "The question is not one of explaining a
language-game by means of experiences, but of noting a language-
game." [2] "Philosophy simply puts everything before us, and
neither explains nor deduces anything." [3] "Philosophy may in
no way interfere with the actual use of language; it can in the
end only describe it." [4]

The task of Husserl's theory of meaning is likewise *not* to help
us in deciding which expressions are meaningful and which not,
but to describe what is meant by saying that an expression is
meaningful. He is neither advancing a criterion, nor is he making
a linguistic proposal. He relies, if we are permitted to say so, on
'ordinary' use and 'ordinary' decision.

Such an attitude is antithetical to any attempt to reduce all
expressions to one favoured type: whether that type be represented by 'protocol' sentences of the logical positivist, or by the
'bloodless categories' of the Hegelian logic. Husserl in this
respect is a pluralist and would make room for what Waismann
has so aptly called "language-strata." Husserl, I guess, would
have given his full assent to Waismann's thesis that statements
are verifiable in radically different senses and so also are
meaningful in radically different senses.[5] But, more of this
later on.

[1] L. Wittgenstein, *Philosophical Investigations*, Oxford, 1953, p. 201.
[2] ibid., p. 167.
[3] .ibid., p. 50.
[4] ibid., p. 49.
[5] A. Flew, *Logic and Language*, Second Series, Oxford, 1955.

§ 9.   Coming now to Husserl's own positive theory of meaning, we could say that the whole theory centres round a certain distinction which he draws between what he calls *'meaning-intention'* and what he calls *'meaning-fulfilment.'* Once we reject the theories which take the meaningfulness of expressions to consist in intuitive experiences (outer or inner), we shall find it possible to explain what should be recognized to be a very fundamental and undeniable distinction, *the distinction between mere thinking or merely symbolical understanding and intuitive apprehension.* For those who take meaningfulness to consist in certain intuitive experiences cannot explain how expressions could be meaningful even when there is complete absence of any such 'corresponding' experience.

Let us consider the following seven expressions, each of which is so chosen as to represent a certain type: (1) *'Abcaderaf,'* (2) *'Roundsquare,'* (3) 'Pegasus,' (4) 'The present King of France,' (5) 'The other side of the moon,' (6) 'Man,' (7) 'This white wall before me,' and (8) Syncategorematic expressions like 'is,' 'or,' 'and.'

(1) is clearly not an expression at all; it is meaningless. 'Roundsquare' (2) is a meaningful expression; only it is absurd that it should designate any entity, the 'corresponding' intuition being *a priori* impossible. 'Pegasus' (3) is also meaningful, and in its case also there is no designatum; the 'corresponding' intuition is ruled out, not a priori but as a matter of fact. 'Pegasus' (3) and 'The present king of France' (4) are so far alike, both being meaningful and both being without any designatum; in both cases the presence of a designatum is ruled out not a priori but as a matter of fact. But there is this difference between them that while no use of 'Pegasus' ever referred to an existent entity, there were uses of 'The present king of France' that did genuinely refer. As contrasted with (3) and (4), 'The other side of the moon' (5) is both meaningful and genuinely referring; only as a matter of fact – again, not a priori – the possibility of 'corresponding' intuition, or of verification, is for the present ruled out. We know however the method of verification. 'Man' (6) is both meaningful and genuinely referential; though it can be genuinely used without being accompanied by 'corresponding' intuition, such 'corresponding' intuition is readily available. (7) however is

such that its meaningful use is always accompanied by 'corresponding' intuition. Syncategorematic expressions (8) are meaningful, though not referential; they are however capable of 'verificatory' experience, of 'corresponding' intuition, though of experience of a kind radically different from sensuous experience.

One way of grasping the distinction between meaning-intention and meaning-fulfilment is by asking: what exactly differentiates (1) from the rest? And what feature characterizes the expressions (2)–(8) in common in spite of their differing referential and verificatory capabilities? Expressions (2) to (8) are animated, according to Husserl, by meaning-intention, whereas the expression (1) lacks it. It is this feature, the meaning-intention, which constitutes the essence of an expression *qua* expression as contrasted with a meaningless string of marks. If we prefer instead the subjective language of a noetic phenomenology, we should say that a genuine expression *qua* expression is constituted by a meaning-intending act. What varies however from case to case with regard to the above-mentioned set of meaningful expressions is the possibility or impossibility (a priori or a posteriori) – and also the precise nature – of meaning-fulfilment. In some cases the meaning-fulfilment through 'corresponding' intuition is ruled out a priori, in some cases it is ruled out as a matter of fact; in some cases again, the meaning-fulfilment is ready at hand while in others it is a matter of graduated achievement. In some cases it is the ordinary sensuous experience, in others it is a type of *Kategorialer* intuition. But all meaningful expressions are meaningful by virtue of the meaning-intention which they embody.

The same distinction could be introduced by asking what distinguishes mere thought from knowledge. I might merely think of a thing without knowing it: my thought of the other side of moon, or of the roundsquare, or even of the prime numbers between 1000 and 2000 does not as such amount to knowledge. Husserl would say that whereas thinking consists in the meaning-intending act, knowing consists in the appropriate fulfilment of the meaning-intention. So long as the meaning-intention is not fulfilled, we do not have knowledge. Knowledge is an intuitive apprehension of what otherwise was only symbolically thought of. And yet the symbolic thought was meaningful. A satisfactory theory of meaning should bear this in mind, and should not confuse between meaning-intention and meaning-fulfilment. This latter confusion is, according to Husserl, the chief error of all imagism and verification-theories.

9.1. Coming now to the controversial notion of 'meaning-intention' we may again connect our exposition with Wittgenstein's *Philosophical Investigations*. It is well-known that the Wittgensteinians would prefer a different answer to the question we have formulated above: 'what distinguishes the expressions (2)–(8) from (1)?' They would suggest that whereas in the case of expressions (2)–(8), there are rules, linguistic conventions etc. for their use, we do not have any such rules or conventions for the use of (1). What makes some signs meaningful is that there are such rules governing their use; what makes some others meaningless is the absence of such rules. We do not know what to do with (1), but we know what to do with (2)–(8). To understand an expression, on this view, is to be able to do something with it, to use it according to rules etc. etc., but *not* to *grasp* some mysterious entity called its meaning. The meaning is its use.

After having said all this, Wittgenstein goes on to ask the really pertinent question: "But we *understand* the meaning of a word when we hear or say it; we grasp it in a flash, and what we grasp in this way is surely something different from the 'use' which is extended in time.[1] "But can the whole *use* of the word come before my mind, when I *understand* it in this way?" [2] One answer to this question is immediately set aside by Wittgenstein. This is the answer that what is present in the mind is a mental picture. "Is there such a thing as a picture, or something like a picture, that forces a particular application on us...?" [3] Wittgenstein rightly rejects this answer, for "the same thing can come before our minds (i.e., the same picture) when we hear the word and the application still be different. Has it the *same* meaning both times? I think we shall say not." [3] The meaning is *not* something

[1] *Philosophical Investigations*, p. 53.
[2] *ibid.*, p. 54.
[3] *ibid.*, p. 55.

that comes before the mind, a picture, a scheme, an image. But again, is there not something *in an expression qua expression* that makes possible an understanding of it *prior to* all application, that in fact predetermines what applications of it would be right applications and what not. 'A set of rules, conventions etc. is all that is needed to do this work,' we shall be told by the Wittgensteinians. But it cannot certainly be said that understanding an expression *is the same as* being aware of such a set of rules, conventions etc. No such rules or conventions are in fact present before the mind. "The application is still a criterion of understanding." [1] But does application also constitute *the nature* of understanding?

To all this it might be replied by saying that although actual application does not constitute the nature of understanding, *applicability* certainly does (which reminds one of the way 'verifiability' was substituted for actual verification). The switch-over to *applicability* (as also to verifiability) only shows that the meaning of an expression cannot be identified with any actual application (or verification) I am making at any moment, that the recourse to the language of possibility is but inevitable, and that understanding *is not* possible application (or verification) but makes right application (or verification) possible.

The idea that meaning *is* applicability is sought to be strengthened by the opinion of many modern philosophers that 'knowing' and 'understanding' *are* capacity words. "The grammar of the word 'knows' is evidently closely related to that of 'can,' 'is able to.' But also closely related to that of 'understands'". [2] Following Wittgenstein, Austin has emphasized the analogy between 'I know' and 'I promise.' I understand when I *can* go on. It is time that this now fashionable view should begin to be suspected. For there is an obvious parallel between the reduction of 'I know' and 'I understand' to 'I can...' and the now almost discarded reduction of categorical material-object statements to hypothetical sense-datum statements. The former reduction shares its strength and weakness with the latter reduction. It has long since been recognized that although a set of hypothetical sense-datum statements *follow* from the truth of a given

[1] *ibid.*, p. 58.
[2] *ibid.*, p. 59.

material-object statement, it is by no means true that the latter statement is equivalent to, i.e. reducible to the former set. Likewise, although it should follow from the statement 'I know ....' that I should be willing or prepared to defend myself when the occasion arises or from the statement 'I understand...' that I should be able to 'go on' when required, it is by no means true that the words 'know' and 'understand' are capacity words or analogous to making promises. Once this point is seen, it would be easy to appreciate that *understanding prior to actual application* must have to be explained in some other way.

Should we then say that the steps to be taken, the uses to be made are "in some *unique* way predetermined, anticipated?" [1] Don't we say that "a machine *has* (possesses) such and such possibilities of movement?" Wittgenstein rightly sees the problem which the positivists who talked about verifiability did not quite see. "What is this possibility of movement?" (or of use, or of verification?), he asks.[2] It is not the actual movement (or the use or the verification). Nor is it "the mere physical conditions for moving either" (nor, the conditions of use or verification). The *supposed* possibility of a movement seems to Wittgenstein to be rather like a shadow of the movement (or of the use or the verification) itself. Meaning then as the possibility of use or verification would be a sort of shadow of actual use or of actual verification. This surely it is not, for not only am I not making an actual use or actual verification, I am not even imagining a shadow of them.

The problem then persists, how to account for our merely symbolic understanding (or 'grasping' the meaning) of an expression *prior to* any actual use, application or verification. We have seen that such understanding cannot consist in entertaining an image, a mental picture, a scheme. It does not also consist in merely having a capacity, a disposition, in making a promise, in a readiness to go on in a certain way, although from the fact that one so understands or grasps, all these do follow. It is also far from being the possession of a shadowy possibility. It must be something actual and concrete. *Husserl's idea of meaning-intention is based on this phenomenological evidence.*

[1] *ibid.*, p. 76.
[2] *ibid.*, p. 78.

9.2.   One major source of troubles in understanding Husserl's philosophy lies in the idea of *'intention.'* It is needless to point out that a psychological interpretation of this term is ruled out in the present context. (Taken psychologically, the statement that an expression embodies a meaning-intention would have meant that behind the physical symbol there stands or works a conscious or unconscious desire or intention to mean such and such by the symbol concerned). There is of course a rough parallel. Just as 'intention' in the psychological sense stands for "what is left over if we subtract the fact that B does *not* occur from the fact that A *fails* to do B" [1] so does 'meaning-intention,' in the present case, stand for the difference between a physical sign and the same sign considered or used as a meaningful expression.

There is no doubt that in interpreting Husserl here we can not but connect what he says about meaning-intention with his general doctrine of the intentionality of consciousness. And further in bringing this connection to light, we begin to realize *the predominance of the noetic approach* over the noematic *in his philosophy of meaning.* For Husserl is *not* saying that a certain impalpable entity inhabits the physical framework of a written or spoken word. Husserl is *not* concerned with the expression considered as an entity; one *cannot* object that Husserl claims to detect within the written or spoken word something that most of us do not see there. *What he is concerned with is the analysis of our experience of meaningfully using an expression.* The analysis which he offers detects two major components of this *experience:* (i) a sensuous awareness of the physical sign and (ii) a peculiar intellectual awareness that transforms a sign into an expression. The first alone does not constitute our awareness or understanding of expressions: so far Husserl and the Wittgensteinians would agree. But whereas according to Husserl there is another descriptive constituent of this awareness or of this understanding, according to Wittgenstein the *experience* involved has no other descriptive constituent except a certain use or operation undertaken. If the actual use or operation undertaken is not adequate – and that it is inadequate is realized by Wittgenstein – we are

[1] R. Chisholm, "Review of Anscombe's Intention," *Philosophical Review*, 1959, p. 112.

to look not for a mental experience but for the peculiar objective "circumstances," [1] which justify me in saying I can go on. "An intention," says Wittgenstein, "is embedded in its situation, in human customs and institutions." [2] If there were no techniques or rules of playing chess, Wittgenstein argues, I could not even intend to play a game of chess. Further, Wittgenstein continues, I can intend the construction of a sentence in advance, only because I can speak the language in question. What does this argument of Wittgenstein prove? It proves, if anything at all, that certain objective circumstances must be given in order that I could even intend in a certain way. The intention does not create the objective conditions, but the objective conditions make the intention possible. (Likewise, one could go on to argue that unless the sense organs are normally constituted and unless there is sufficient illumination etc., one cannot have a visual perception. But is this a relevant point at all so far as theory of perception is concerned? Certainly not. The physiological and other objective conditions that make visual perception possible are not descriptive constituents of that perception itself.) The fact that a conventional system of signs with rules of operation known as a language must be given in order that I could even intend constructing a sentence, does not decide any of the philosophical issues confronting us. Husserl is not denying that the system of *signs* that goes to constitute a language is the product of association and therefore of custom. But that is for him not a sufficient reason for holding the view that a linguistic expression is nothing other than such a sign or that our understanding of an expression is nothing other than the capacity to operate with the sign in accordance with custom-bred conventions. It should further have been noticed that the intention which Wittgenstein finds imbedded in objective circumstances and therefore as worthless is not the same as Husserl's meaning-intention.

Husserl's contention therefore would be that, given a set of signs and rules of operation developed through custom, such a set with its rules would not amount to a *language* (nor would their use amount to an *understanding*) unless the said intellectual

---

[1] *Op. cit.*, p. 60.
[2] *ibid.*, p. 108.

act – the meaning-intending act – supervened. This is the reason why the 'games' invented or imagined by Wittgen**stein** would not be called 'languages,' unless this condition is fulfilled, and when this condition *is* fulfilled, they cease to be mere 'games.'

Saying that an intellectual act of awareness is essential for our experience of meaningfully using (or for understanding) an expression does *not* necessarily amount to saying that in case of such understanding, we *inspect* the intentional correlate of that act. The latter contention cannot therefore be advanced as a valid charge against Husserl. Husserl in fact warns us against such a misconstruction. Husserl tells us [1] that in meaning-intending acts we are not objectively (*gegenständlich*) aware of the meanings. When judging, we judge not about the meaning of the expression but about the state of affairs referred to. It is only in a subsequent act of reflection that we may come to be objectively aware of the meaning of the expression, the proposition, as distinguished from the state of affairs referred to. If Platonism is, according to a formulation by White, the view "that the mental activity called understanding is one in which we grasp meanings conceived as non-mental, non-physical entities," [2] Husserl's theory of thinking is certainly not Platonistic. But it is certainly Platonistic in a much better sense, as we shall try to show in the following sections.

The reproach that the phenomenologist's attempt to detect meanings everywhere and in all forms of discourse leads to a logicism that misses the logic of actual living speech is not also any more justified. But an exact defence of Husserl against this reproach would be undertaken in a later section in which we shall be concerned with Husserl's attitude towards language in general.

§ 10.   After having attempted a statement and a defence of Husserl's notion of 'meaning-intention,' let us now turn to the correlative notion of 'meaning-fulfilment.' We have seen that the notion of 'meaning-intention' is called for to account for our understanding of expressions even in the absence of the appropriate verificatory experiences; in other words, it is meant

[1] *L.U.*, II, 1, First Investigation, § 34.
[2] M. White, *Reunion in Philosophy*, p. 192.

to explain what has been called merely symbolic understanding or thought. It is meant to account for that 'grasping in a flash' which precedes, and also makes possible the variegated and varying uses an expression is capable of. We could likewise say that the correlative notion of meaning-fulfilment is called for to account for the *difference* between mere thought or *symbolic understanding* on the one hand and *knowledge* on the other. If one way of clarifying a notion is to assimilate it to another with which we are more familiar, then we could suggest that the idea of meaning-fulfilment is meant to absorb all that is valuable in the positivist's notion of verification, after rectifying his errors and lapses and thereby making room for different levels of verification.

10.1. It has been pointed out that verifiability fails as a criterion of meaningfulness and that in fact the very notion of a criterion of meaningfulness suffers from a fundamental error. Expressions are meaningful prior to, and independently of actual verification. Their meaningfulness is independent even of their verifiability. This is not however to deny that the meaning of an expression bears an important relation to verificatory experience. How is this relationship to be formulated? Bradley who cautioned us against taking meaning as imaging ended up however with a compromise: the meaning, he held, is nevertheless a part of the content of the image, only as abstracted from its psychical existence at the moment. It was an easy game for Blanshard [1] to expose this Bradleyan compromise with psychologism, and we may safely take it as a settled point that this is not the way one ought to formulate the relation between meaning and verification. The relation of part and whole is as much inapplicable as that of a property to its criterion.

Now, according to Husserl, the relationship is best described as that of 'intention' to 'fulfilment,' both terms being understood on the *barest analogy* of the corresponding psychological experiences.

Understanding, according to the analysis of the foregoing section, is the grasping or re-living of the meaning-intention. Thinking also is basically – that is to say, regarding that com-

[1] See § 8.1.(i) above.

ponent of it which underlies, makes possible and also supplements our operation with symbols – a meaning-intending act, a peculiarly original form of awareness.

In the widest sense of course all awareness is intentional. Awareness is awareness *of* something. But within the class of all intentional acts there is a narrower group to which the so-called meaning-intending *acts* [1] belong. Thinking, in other words, is intentional in a sense that is more specific than the broader sense in which all awareness is said to be so. In this specific sense, the title 'Intention' serves to circumscribe a class of experiences "which are characterized by the peculiarity of being capable of founding fulfilling-relationships." [2] Thought, though belonging to this narrower class of intentional experiences, does not constitute this class by itself; there are other intentional acts belonging to this group as well, and it shall serve our purpose to bring to light the peculiarity they all share in common before returning to the sort of experience with which we are primarily concerned.

It has been said that in the case of thought the relationship Intention-fulfilment has to be understood on the barest analogy of the corresponding psychological experiences; and notwithstanding all anti-psychologism of the phenomenologist, such an analogy is indispensable. In fact we may arrange the experiences that are intentional in this more specific sense in a serial order such that the preceding members of the series would be more psychological than the succeeding ones. In other words, advancing in this series we would gradually liberate the sense of the fulfilment-relationship from direct psychologism and should have to satisfy ourselves more and more with the bare analogy. Consider, to start with, the case nearest to psychology: desire or wish-intention and its fulfilment or frustration. Take as a next example one's experience of listening to a known melody: as soon as one hears the initial move, there are awakened definite

[1] Let it be noted, with a view to warding off a common objection once for ever, that Husserl uses the word 'Act' to stand for all intentional experiences, and that he explicitly rejects the "Mythology of activities." (see *L.U.*, II, 1, pp. 378–379, especially p. 379 f).

[2] *L.U.*, II, 2, p. 39. See also *L.U.*, II, 1, pp. 378–379. In the broader sense, even the fulfilling experiences, like all experiences, are intentional; but the fulfilling experiences are *not* intentional in the narrower sense, i.e. in the sense of making possible further fulfilling experiences.

intentions which come to be fulfilled only step by step with the progress of the melody. In both these cases, the relationship lies close to that between an expectation and its fulfilment, whereas it should be noted that this is not so in all cases of intention and of its fulfilment. Intention, even in this specific sense, is *not* expectation, is *not* to-be-directed-towards-the-future.[1] When I see an incomplete picture, say of a carpet partly hidden by a piece of furniture, what I see of course carries an intention which points towards completion, although we do not expect anything. In case of our perception of physical objects, likewise, what we apprehend, i.e. what are given to us point towards the features that are not given; perceptual acts are thus intentional inasmuch as they make possible further perceptual acts. Furthest removed from a psychological interpretation is the intention involved in the acts of thinking and understanding.

Among intentional acts in this narrower sense, Husserl distinguishes between two radically different groups. To the one group belong the desire and wish intentions. The other group consists in what Husserl calls the objectfying (*objektivierenden*) acts. An act is said to be an 'objectifying' one if it is capable of functioning as a component of a knowledge situation. Knowledge, as distinguished from mere thought, consists in an intuitive fulfilment of an intention accompanied by a consciousness of the identity of the fulfilment with the intention. In other words, it is a fulfilment that identifies itself with the intention. We could therefore say that objectifying acts are those that *are capable of* such identifying fulfilment. Meaning-intention belongs to this group of objectifying intentional acts.[2]

The objectifying acts are capable of further classification into the *signitive* or symbolic [3] and the *intuitive* acts, the distinction between them corresponding to that between thought and intuition.[4] Signitive intentions constitute the meaning of expressions. It is however important to bear in mind that intuitive acts – perceptual or imaginative – are capable of further fulfilment and that therefore even intuitive acts may contain unfulfilled intentions within them. This happens, e.g., in the

[1] *L.U.*, II, 1, p. 40.
[2] *L.U.*, II, 2, pp. 51–52.
[3] *L.U.*, II, 2, p. 33 f.
[4] *L.U.*, II, 2, pp. 53–56.

case of perception of physical objects, as mentioned above.

The above classification of intentional acts may be represented as follows:

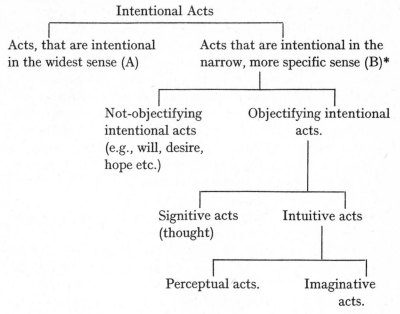

Intentional Acts

Acts, that are intentional in the widest sense (A)

Acts that are intentional in the narrow, more specific sense (B)*

Not-objectifying intentional acts (e.g., will, desire, hope etc.)

Objectifying intentional acts.

Signitive acts (thought)

Intuitive acts

Perceptual acts.

Imaginative acts.

[*The group of acts (B), it is obvious, is a sub-class included within the group (A)].

10.2.   Two preliminary points about the intention-fulfilment situation should be mentioned at this stage in order to avoid further misunderstanding: first, the meaning-intention is not an indefinite, indeterminate character waiting to be first determined and made definite by the fulfilling experience.[1] On the other hand, it is always, in each case, already something determinate and specific, even prior to verification. In the second place it must be clearly seen that the relation between intention and fulfilment is not external. The relation could perhaps be better expressed by saying that the fulfilment is fulfilment precisely of *this* intention, and, conversely, that *this* intention pre-determines its possible fulfilment.

The second of the above two statements needs explication.

[1] *L.U.*, II, 1, p. 98.

And I must confess I find no better means of explicating Husserl's point than by referring to a rather well-known doctrine of the American idealist philosopher Josiah Royce. Royce distinguished between what he called the 'internal meaning' of an idea and its 'external meaning.' The difficulty that he felt about the commonsense notion that the meaning of an idea was either the external object referred to or the corresponding verificatory experience is genuine. How can you, unless you have a prior understanding of the idea, know that any given external object is the object of *this* idea, or that the verificatory experience verifies, or corresponds to, precisely *this* idea? Besides, he also felt that there is no generalized pattern of correspondence relation which could hold good between an idea and its object in all cases: the relation between the idea of 'man' and a 'corresponding' image or perception is different from the relation between a mathematical representation of a physical phenomenon and a 'corresponding' image or perception of it. There is no one standard by which we could decide in any case that an object is the object of this idea or that an experience verifies this idea. Faced with this genuine difficulty, Royce suggested in a rather obsolete metaphorical-metaphysical language that the idea selects its own object. What he meant is partly that it is only after understanding an idea, i.e. grasping the meaning-intention that we can recognize an object as *its* object or an experience as its corresponding experience. Royce no doubt meant many other things besides. He did hold that thinking was purposive, that our intellectual activities are basically voluntaristic, that every idea embodies a purpose which finds fulfilment, as he also said, in the outer experience. There was also his Hegelian belief that an Absolute purpose manifested itself through these finite purposes and was seeking fulfilment in finite experience. Now, we are not at all interested here in Royce's metaphysics. The point that interests us is the genuine difficulty he felt and the important phenomenological distinction he drew between the 'intended meaning' and the 'external meaning' which is the fulfilment of that intention. Shorn of Royce's Absolutism and also of his voluntarism, this distinction comes as near to Husserl's doctrine as any other view held by any other philosopher.

Royce's difficulty is solved by maintaining that the 'internal meaning' determines the 'external meaning.' In Husserl's language, the meaning-intention which, as we said, is already determinate further determines the range and the type of fulfilment it is capable of. Only by grasping a meaning-intention, I can recognize an experience as its fulfilment.

10.3. The relation between a meaning-intention and its fulfilment is not however of an uniform type as the foregoing analysis might make it appear to be. On the contrary, there are various types of this relation. To start with, one may distinguish between static and dynamic unities [1] of intention and fulfilment. In the case of knowledge, where the thought and the intuition are already together, their unity is static: both are given in a static relation of identity. On the other hand, one may start with a mere thought, with a merely 'signitive' meaning-intention, and *then pass over to* the fulfilling intention: that would be a case of dynamic unity. In static unity, intention and fulfilment are temporally coincident, in dynamic unity they come one after another.

The dynamic fulfilment may take the form of a graduated process of approximation towards an ideally perfect knowledge. In other words the fulfilment may not come all at once, but may emerge in the form of a graduated and ascending series. An ideally perfect fulfilment would be an experience in which the object is given, intuited, exactly as it was meant in the signitive or symbolic meaning-intention. There is of course another sense [2] in which one can speak of absolute fulfilment. In this sense, the fulfilling intuition shall not harbour any further unfulfilled intention demanding fulfilment. It is obvious that one has to fall back upon the absolutely given in perception. Turning now to the list given in § 9, we may conclude with the following remarks:

'Abcaderaf' (i) is no expression, for it carries (i.e., awakens in us) no meaning-intention.

'Roundsquare' (2) carries a meaning-intention which is *a priori* incapable of fulfilment.

[1] *L.U.*, II, 2, § 6, § 8.
[2] *L.U.*, II, 2, pp. 118-119.

'Pegasus' (3) carries a meaning-intention whose *absolute* fulfilment is *a posteriori* ruled out; an imaginative fulfilment nevertheless is possible.

'The present king of France' (4) is so far like (3), but is unlike it in so far as it *was* at one time capable of actual fulfilment although as used by any one *now* its meaning-intention is incapable of fulfilment.

'The other side of the moon'(5) has a meaning-intention capable of fulfilment which however is hindered by present circumstances.

'Man' (6) has a meaning-intention capable of fulfilment, static or dynamic.

'This white wall before me' (7), however, is such that its meaning-intention must be a component in the static unity of knowledge; in other words, its meaningful use must be accompanied by corresponding intuition.

Expressions like 'is,' 'or,' 'and' (8) are meaningful, and their meaning-intentions are capable only of a peculiar type of fulfilment to be discussed in section § 17.1.

Fulfilment or verification, as mentioned before, may be of various types.

§ 11.   Corresponding to the two *acts*, the meaning-intending act and the meaning-fulfilling act, we may speak of the *contents* of those acts which respectively are the intended meaning and the fulfilled meaning. Meaning-intention is an act, an awareness; so also is meaning-fulfilment. But when we speak the language of entities, when we speak of the meaning in the substantive, we refer equivocally to the content of either of these acts. Husserl's Platonism concerns the intended meaning, just as his intellectualism concerns the meaning-intending act. At the same time, it must not be forgotten that there is a positivistic and empiricistic trend in Husserl, and this concerns, in the present context, the other form of awareness i.e. the meaning-fulfilling act and the content of that act, i.e. the fulfilled meaning.

11.1.   Postponing for the next chapter a proper evaluation of the Platonistic trend in Husserl, let us conclude the present one with a summary of our main arguments:

Having discussed the referring function of expressions in the foregoing chapter, we turned our attention to the meaning function, which is the most essential function of expressions qua expressions (§ 7). The Image theory of meaning was at first rejected (§ 7). This led us to a discussion of the false theories of abstraction which are found in the British empiricists Locke, Berkeley, Hume and Mill (§ 7.1.). Husserl's final criticism of Nominalism was recalled in that connection: the main point of it seems to be that the nominalist misses the radical difference that subsists between sensing of particulars and thinking of generalities, the radical difference in the modes of consciousness and in the modes of intending (§ 7.2.). This negative discussion led to the more positive step of distinguishing between an expression considered as a physical event and an expression considered as such, i.e. as an ideal structure. It was emphasized that this distinction is indispensable for any theory of meaning to start with (§ 8). The inner experience theory, or the mental picture theory was rejected (§ 8.1.). Attention was then drawn to remarkable similarities between Wittgenstein (of the *Philosophical Investigations*) and Husserl. Both reject the inner experience or mental picture theory, and both reject the idea of a criterion of meaningfulness (§ 8.2.). Husserl, it was pointed out, would rather welcome Waismann's conception of different levels of verification (§ 8.2.). Coming now to Husserl's own positive theory of meaning, we found that the theory centres round the distinction between 'meaning-intention' and 'meaning-fulfilment.' The idea of 'meaning-intention,' we found, is introduced to account for our understanding of expressions prior to, or even in the absence of, verificatory experience (§ 9), just as the correlative notion of meaning-fulfilment is meant to account for the difference between merely symbolic understanding and knowledge (§ 10). With regard to meaning-intention, the central question was formulated and discussed in the language of Wittgenstein thus: is there an understanding, a grasping of the intention prior to actual verification or application? Understanding is neither actual application nor applicability (§ 9.1.). Husserl's conception of meaning-intention was claimed to be based on genuine phenomenological evidence. But how to interpret this notion? An analogy with the psychological notion is unavoidable, but one should avoid psychologism. In any case,

Husserl's interest is primarily noetic: he is primarily concerned with our *experience* of meaningfully using expressions. This experience, according to him, has an intellectual component which supervenes upon the sensuous and the operational. But Husserl is *not* saying that we inspect a subsistent entity; living an act is not inspecting the object of that act (§ 9.2.). The relation between intention and fulfilment was likewise sought to be freed from psychologism, although here as before the analogy with the psychological was found to be unavoidable (§ 10.1.). Husserl's theory was explained with reference to Royce's distinction between 'external meaning' and 'internal meaning' (§ 10.2.). The fulfilment of a meaning-intention may be static or dynamic, all at once or graduated (§ 10.3.). Knowledge is the fulfilment of an intention accompanied by a consciousness of identification or adequacy. Finally, the distinction between the two forms of awareness, the meaning-intending and the meaning-fulfilling, leads to a further distinction between the contents of those acts, the language of entities being concerned only with the latter (§ 11).

It hardly needs to be recalled at this stage that we have given reasons why the operationalist theory of meaning is not acceptable to us.

11.2. We cannot, however, conclude the chapter without disentangling a complication. Leaving aside the pronouncing function and taking into consideration the referring and the meaning functions, we have distinguished between:

(*a*) the reference,
(*b*) the meaning-intention,
and (*c*) the meaning-fulfilment
of an expression.

Corresponding to the three functions, we have spoken of three entities:

(*a'*) the object referred to,
(*b'*) the intended meaning,
and (*c'*) the fulfilled meaning.

The relation between (*a*) and (*b*) has been touched upon in § 6.2. But what precisely is the relation between (a) and (c), and between (a') and (c')? It seems as if there is no direct relation, indirect relation though there may be. Since the mode of reference is determined by meaning-intention, and since fulfilment is fulfilment of intention, (a) and (c), and therefore (a') and (c') must also be related with each other.

The relation, however, is closer than that. The reference to the object is said to be 'realised' [1] when the object is given either in actual perception or in imagination. When the reference is unrealized, it is said to be enclosed (*beschlossen*) in the mere meaning-intention. "As the empty meaning-intention fulfils itself, the objective reference is realized and naming becomes an actual conscious relation between the name and the named." [2] "The meaningful expression is unified with the act of meaning-fulfilment in the realized relation of the expression to its object."

Thus we find that the realization of the reference, i.e., the presentation or representation of the object referred to and the fulfilment of the meaning-intention are but two sides of the same phenomenon.

Since the reference is conditioned by the meaning-intention, the object referred to is to be given by way of fulfilment of that intention and therefore the mode of givenness of the object of reference is conditioned by the meaning-intention itself.

This does not however entitle us to go a step ahead and say that the object of reference is *the same* as the meaning-fulfilment: for that would commit us to a sort of *phenomenalism* which is *not* phenomenologically sound.

[1] *L.U.*, II, 1, p. 37.
[2] *L.U.*, II, 1, p. 38.

CHAPTER IV

HUSSERL'S PHILOSOPHY OF LANGUAGE

§ 12.   We have said that Husserl's *Platonism*, in his theory of meaning, concerns the intended meaning or the content of the meaning-intending act, whereas his *positivism* concerns the fulfilled meaning or the content of the meaning-fulfilling act. It is the intended meaning of which the language of *entities* holds good; besides, it is of the intended meaning that we can predicate that identity, objectivity and universality, in short, that ideality which Platonists ascribe to the socalled abstract entities. On the other hand, the idea of meaning-fulfilment seeks to accommodate the phenomenological element in the positivist's emphasis on empirical verification. Thus Husserl may be said to have brought about a synthesis of Platonism and Anti-Platonism, the two opposed camps who have fought the battle over the problem of 'meaning.'

12.1.   Both the camps have their respective merits and drawbacks. Platonism has caught hold of one of those fundamental phenomena which any satisfactory theory of meaning must take into account: the fact that thought transcends the privacy of one's mind and is essentially communicable and shareable, that expressions retain a degree of identity of meaning in discourse (for, otherwise thought would lack communicability and logical thinking would be an impossibility), that thought is not mere construction but is also a mode of disclosure. Likewise, the anti-Platonists, scared of ontological hypostatisation of abstract impalpable entities, emphasise the other indisputable phenomenon: the fact that meaningful discourse has an unavoidable reference to experience in which our thought finds its final consummation and fulfilment.

Their drawbacks are equally obvious. Platonism fails to

connect the hypostatised meanings with the thinking mind on the one hand and the empirical reference on the other. Psychologism fails to account for that identity in discourse, objectivity, and shareability which cannot be denied of meanings.

(i) In the preceding chapter we have examined *the operationalist variety of anti-Platonism* and have adduced reasons for rejecting it. Operationalism however has the one unmistakable merit that it is able to account for the objectivity and sharability of meaning, for the theory could explain these features by appealing to the rules of operation accepted in common by those who use the language in question, rules which are not private to any thinking mind. But, as we pointed out in the last chapter, it cannot satisfactorily account for our understanding prior to actual operation, use or application; to fall back on expectation would be going back to psychologism, and to take recourse to applicability or capacity would be to take one's refuge under a dubious shelter, for a proper interpretation of dispositional words would threaten the theory itself.

Before returning to our central theme, we shall briefly refer in this section to a few more attempts either to improve upon psychologism or to avoid Platonism.

(ii) Stevenson in his *Ethics and Language* (Yale, 1944) attempts to avoid the unstability of psychologism without at the same time taking meanings as any sort of entities. Stevenson rightly sees that the problem is to find an invariant amidst psychological flux. Psychological reactions to an expression (as to, let us say, coffee) fluctuate. But one could speak of a 'disposition,' a 'power,' a 'potentiality' (just as we say, 'coffee has a stimulating power') that is something relatively stable. In order to get at the relative stability of meaning, Stevenson undertakes an analysis of the concepts of 'disposition' and 'power.' A disposition is neither a special object that exists over and above, behind and beyond its tangible manifestations, nor is it the *cause* of the actual responses. Avoiding these possibilities, Stevenson attempts to define 'disposition' *in use*, which involves details that need not be followed up here. Granted that such a definition were possible, it becomes relatively easy to say what meaning is. Meaning, in that case, is a *dispositional property of the sign*. This dispositional property is relatively stable while the actual responses vary.

In its metaphysical form, the idea of 'power' has been made use of by some of the ancient Indian systems to explain the *relation* between a word and its meaning. But to reduce meaning itself to this power or disposition – even if 'disposition' be defined in use – is highly questionable. For to mention only the most important reason, disposition or power, on any interpretation, is not felt as being given; it is either *inferred* as a metaphysical entity or only *constructed* out of actual responses elicited. But in any case it is not felt to be given or apprehended as such in primary experience. Meaning however is felt to be given and not to be inferred or constructed. What is felt to be given cannot be reduced to what is inferred or merely constructed.

(iii) While Stevenson has tried to improve upon psychologism, Quine,[1] as is well-known, has suggested *measures for avoiding Platonism*. Three of these measures may be mentioned here. First, by keeping 'meaning' and 'reference' strictly separate we can exclude all questions about entities from the theory of meaning altogether. Secondly, the main problem in the theory of meaning would then centre around the concepts of synonymity and analyticity. Finally, there is the purely technical device of imposing certain restrictions against quantifying over functions and abstract entities with the help of which Quine seeks to eliminate Platonism from the ontological commitments of logic.

The last of these three measures does not directly concern theory of meaning. What concerns us here is the question, whether the distinction between meaning and reference can successfully eliminate the language of entities from the theory of meaning.

The discussions of the preceding chapters must have shown that the matter is not as simple as Quine takes it to be. It would be a gross over-simplification to suggest that the Platonic theory of meaning is based on a confusion between meaning and reference. On the other hand, by excluding from consideration the objects referred to, attention may be fixed on meanings as such, i.e. on the immanent contents of thought in their selfidentities: that would lead to *the really genuine* form of Platonism in the theory of meaning. Quine's own discussions, as well as those of White and Waismann, of the concepts of synonymity and analyticity

[1] W. V. O. Quine, *From a Logical Point of View*, Harvard, 1953.

have shown that there are only two alternatives from which we
are to choose: – either recognize sameness of meaning as too
fundamental a feature to be explained by any notion other than
itself; or, if you demand an external criterion of sameness, you
won't find it and then dismiss the concepts of synonymity and
analyticity as spurious. Quine, White, and many others choose
the second alternative; Husserl would choose the first. If there
is any point in Quine's argument,[1] it is not that we do not know
or cannot know that a given proposition is analytic, but that we
cannot adduce sufficient reasons *why* it is so. As Taylor has
pointed out,[2] the difficulty is inherent in any question of a
criterion of *sameness*. Even in the absence of such a criterion,
phenomenology would not be prepared to defy the evidence of
phenomena and deny so fundamental a feature of our intellectual
life.

(iv) Philosophers often deny the importance of what we have
just characterized as a fundamental feature of our intellectual
life. No word of language has a fixed objective meaning, it will
be pointed out. The so-called invariable objective meaning, it
has been said,[3] is only an abstraction, cut off from the living
linguistic meaning, from that "immanent dialectic" which
characterizes actual conversation between persons. Without
such artificial sundering, there would be no identical meanings,
no ideal meaning-unities.

Whorf's paper on *"Language, Mind and Reality"* [4] draws our
attention to the same situation though from a quite different
metaphysical background. According to Whorf, language has
two aspects: the "patternment"-aspect and the lexicographic
or name-giving aspect. In the latter aspect, language gives
names to parts of a whole, isolates them, fixes them as if they
were self-subsisting entities. In the former aspect, language is
concerned, neither with 'names' and 'forms,' nor with definite
spatio-temporal organisations, but with pure patternments.

[1] W. V. O. Quine, "Two dogmas of empiricism," *The Philosophical Review*, 1951,
pp. 20–43.

[2] R. Taylor, "Disputes about synonymy," *The Philosophical Review*, 1954, pp. 517–
529.

[3] H. Lipps, *Untersuchungen zu einer hermeneutischen Logik*, Frankfurt, 1938. This
work anticipates many of the ideas of Wittgenstein's *Philosophical Investigations*.

[4] Originally published in *The Theosophist*, 1942, now included in Whorf, *Language,
Thought and Reality*, ed. by J. B. Carrol, M.I.T., 1956.

The referring-function which dominates language in its name-giving aspect is at a minimum in the higher, the patternment aspect. In this higher aspect, Whorf maintains, language is algebraic in nature; 'sentences, not words are the essence of speech just as equations and functions, not bare numbers are the real meat of mathematics." [1]

These views, reminiscent of much of Ryle and later Wittgenstein, are based on the following contentions: –

(1) Most words change their meanings from context to context. Besides, there are *essentially ambiguous* expressions including the so-called 'indexical' expressions or 'ego-centric particulars.'

(2) Language consists in actual speaking and hearing, in living conversation, and meanings arise only in this context of speaker-hearer relationship. How could one tear them off from this living context?

(3) The inner reality of language consists in a pure "patternment," and certainly not in that name-giving aspect which comes to the forefront due to the limitations of our practical interests.

The following remarks may serve to clarify our positions with regard to these three points: –

The ambiguity and fluctuations in meaning referred to in (1) may be shown to be due rather to the imperfections of our language systems than to the non-existence of identical meaning-contents. For, though a seemingly identical expression may convey different meanings in different contexts, it is yet theoretically possible to take hold of each such meaning and tie it to one expression. The fluctuations would then be seen to be not of meanings themselves but of the *use* of an *apparently* identical physical expression.

Further, it could be admitted that in its purely formal aspect language exhibits a patternment which is roughly the same as its syntactical aspect. So far as this aspect is concerned, the semantical considerations of the 'material' meaning-contents and of reference are irrelevant. But at the same time it could also be claimed that in a theory concerned precisely with the 'material' aspects of meaning and reference, the 'patternment' aspect is no more illuminating.

---

[1] *The Theosophist*, 1942, p. 27.

The second of the above three contentions places before any Platonic theory of meaning *an almost* insurmountable difficulty. But still it could be argued that the relativity implied in the speaker-hearer relationship is not an inescapable one. This might be worked out in the following way. The meaning situation may be viewed either from the standpoint of the hearer or from that of the speaker. It may be argued however that the speaker's standpoint is more fundamental,[1] that the expression as spoken is the basic phenomenon, that the hearer understands it *as if* he were speaking it, and that therefore the expression *as heard* may be reduced to the expression *as spoken*. If this be so then the two-sided relativity is broken, so that the meaning of an expression as spoken may now be isolated from the act of speaking as its intended content and shown to have that ideality which Platonism ascribes to it.

§ 13.   The discussion of Anti-Platonism in the above section has led us to the fringes of philosophy of language, and it is worth while to thrash out Husserl's concluding attitude towards language before undertaking a final evaluation of his Platonism. As before, a correct appreciation of Husserl here requires placing his thought against the canvas of contemporary philosophical interest in language, and for this purpose a short historical digression may not be superfluous.

Merleau-Ponty in his fascinating study on the phenomenology of language [2] draws our attention to two phases in Husserl's philosophy of language. In the *Logische Untersuchungen*, according to Merleau-Ponty, Husserl suggests the idea of an ideal language and of a universal grammar which would determine the forms of signification indispensable for any language if it is to be a language at all, so that the empirical languages could be regarded as the mixed and disordered (*brouillés*) 'realisations' of that essential or eidetic language. On the other hand, Merleau-Ponty reminds us, Husserl in his very recent texts seems to be taking language as an original mode of disclosure of certain objects: speech is conceived as a process as it were of concreti-

---

[1] It may be noted here that much discussion in Indian philosophy regarding the problem of meaning takes the standpoint of the hearer.

[2] "Sur la phénoménologie du langage," *Problèmes actuels de la phénoménologie*, Bruxelles, 1952.

zation (*Verleiblichung*) of what would remain otherwise a merely intersubjective, ideal structure. When speaking, writes Husserl, *"vollziehen wir fortlaufend ein inneres, sich mit Worten verschmelzendes, sie gleichsam beseelendes Meinen."* [1]

The distinction between these two phases of Husserl's philosophy of language may be regarded as corresponding to the distinction between the objective and the phenomenological attitudes towards language emphasized by Pos. [2] The phenomenological attitude implies a return to the speaking subject, to my contact with the language I speak: from this point of view, Merleau-Ponty reminds us, language is not any more the resultant of a chaotic past of independent linguistic facts, but a system whose elements all converge towards an effort at unique expression, governed by *une logique actuelle*. The distinction between these two phases is only the reflection, in this sphere of problem, of a distinction that permeates Husserl's thought in general, i.e. the distinction between the earlier (or, the middle?) 'eidetic' phase and the later return to the constitutive analysis. Perhaps one could add a concluding phase, signifying the return to the *Lebenswelt* which is nothing but a discovery of yet another dimension of the constitutive analysis.

As in the case of Husserl's thought in general, so here too a true understanding should proceed not by separating these two phases and setting up an irreconcilable opposition between them, but by seeing that these two phases, by correcting and supplementing each other, contribute towards a finally satisfactory philosophical position. It may perhaps be remarked that this would not only help us towards a better understanding of Husserl, but would also contribute towards reconciling the hostile camps into which present day philosophy of language is divided.

13.1.   In the 'eidetic' phase of his philosophy of language Husserl advances two major theses: (*a*) the conception of the ideality of language (*die Idealität des Sprachlichen*) and (*b*) the idea of a pure grammar. The clearest statement of the former is found in the *Formale und Transzendentale Logik*, although the conception lies imbedded in the discussions on expressions and

[1] *F.u.t.L.*, p. 20.

[2] "Phénoménologie et linguistique," *Revue Internationale de philosophie*, 1939.

meaning in the *Logische Untersuchungen*. The second of the two theses is elaborated in the Fourth Logical Investigation.

(*a*) The conception of the ideality of language [1] is based on the distinction between the actually spoken language (*die aktuell geredete Rede*) and the linguistic expression in itself. The former is always a transitory particular, an acoustic event or a visual datum, while the latter alone is repeatable. When therefore we say or write or use the same expression, the identity refers to the latter and not to the former. For, taken strictly in the sense of an actually written or spoken word or sentence, the same expression can never occur twice, and every time we say we are using the same expression in this sense we are only making use of similar expressions. And yet we do speak of the same expression, just as we speak of the same symphony, of the same novel, etc. in spite of different physical reproductions. Thus the expression-in-itself is no more a real transitory event, but an ideal entity or figure which is reproduced, exemplified etc. in the various real events. Its ideality, Husserl goes on to add, is that of an objective spiritual entity (*objektives geistiges Gebilde*). In this sense, its ideality is to be distinguished from that of the thought – or, meaning – expressed by it.[2] The ideality belongs to a linguistic expression even in its purely linguistic aspect (*hinsichtlich der sprachlichen Leiblichkeit*).

It is clear that Husserl is thereby attributing two kinds of ideality to a linguistic expression: the one concerns the expression in its purely linguistic aspect, that is to say in its very corporeal aspect, and the other, of course, concerns its meaning. Part of Husserl's problem is quite the same as that for the solution of which modern semanticists have distinguished between the type-word and the token-word, and the ideality of an expression considered in its corporeal aspect is nothing but the ideality of an expression considered as a type. If the notion of type could account for the phenomenon of repetition of the same expression, the notion of ideality is uncalled for. There is of course a "recognizable pattern" which is "partly a matter of physical similarity and partly a matter of

[1] *F.u.t.L.* § 2; Compare § 8 above.
[2] *F.u.t.L.*, p. 19.

conventional understanding." [1] The difficulty with the notion of ideality in *"rein sprachlicher Hinsicht"* is this: how can the notion of identity be applied to an expression in its *purely* corporeal aspect? One could only detect similarities in pattern. If one speaks of the *same* expression, one can do so not with regard to its purely corporeal aspect, but only in so far as the corporeal aspect is undistinguished from the meaning-aspect. (Considered in the corporeal aspect, what similarity – not to speak of identity - could be there between a written word and the *same* word as spoken?) The ideality of language really concerns the meaning-aspect; in so far, the ideality of language is different from the ideality of non-linguistic works of art, say of a piece of music! It is not possible therefore to agree with Husserl when he says [2] that the ideality of a linguistic expression is different from that of the thought expressed by it.

(*b*) Whereas the notion of the *Idealität des Sprachlichen* concerns each linguistic expression considered by itself – be it a word, a sentence, or even a whole work – the notion of a pure Grammar concerns language as a whole. Further, it concerns not any specific language taken by itself, but all languages, in fact *any* language. We could also say that this notion concerns any language *in so far as* its *a priori* form is concerned. Husserl seems to be of the opinion that although each language has developed-through its own peculiar historical, sociological and environmental circumstances and has its own distinctive peculiarities, nevertheless it does – and in fact it must – conform to an apriori *structure: "an dieses ideale Gerüst ist jede gebunden"*. "The language has not only its physiological, psychological, and ethnological fundamentals, but also its apriori fundamentals." [3] This a priori fundamental consists in the "essential forms of meaning and the a priori laws of their complexities and respective modifications," so that "no language is thinkable which is not determined essentially by this apriori." [3]

What Husserl has in his mind is certainly *not* the notion of an eidetic or ideal *language* of which the empirical languages are imperfect realisations. Merleau-Ponty is wrong when he attri-

[1] C. I. Lewis, "The Modes of Meaning," Linsky, *loc. cit.*, pp. 50–51.
[2] *F.u.t.L.*, p. 19.
[3] *L.U.*, II, 1, p. 338.

butes to Husserl such a conception of an *ideal* language. The peculiarity of Husserl's thought, as we shall point out in the sequel, lies not in distinguishing between an ideal language and the empirical languages (this distinction he did not in reality draw), but in attributing ideality, as we saw in (*a*) above, even to expressions in the empirical languages. What Husserl here suggests is the notion of an a priori universal *grammar* (a grammar is not a language and a language is more than a form) which would, in the words of Merleau-Ponty, "determine the forms of signification indispensable for all languages, if they are to be languages." [1]

13.2. The other i.e. the 'constitutive' phase of Husserl's philosophy of language can already be detected in the very same paragraph of the *Formale und transzendentale Logik* in which he speaks of the *Idealität des Sprachlichen*. With regard to this phase, we might further distinguish between two distinct movements. There is an attempt to trace language back in the first place to the noetic act which makes it possible, and then in the second place to the more primitive *Lebenswelt*. The significance of both these movements has to be brought to light.

(*a*) The unity of the physical expression and the meaning it embodies is not a merely external unity. Rather, "while speaking we perform an inner act of meaning which mingles itself with the words and at the same time animates them" ("*redend vollziehen wir fortlaufend ein inneres, sich mit Worten verschmelzendes, sie gleichsam beseelendes Meinen*").[2] From the point of his constitution-analysis, Husserl is interested not in the objective phenomenon of linguistic expression but in my *experience of language* as I speak it. This problem again is inseparable from the wider question of the possibility of experience in general.[3] Since all experience has a noetic aspect and a noematic aspect, and since

---

[1] Compare Wittgenstein's extended notion of grammar: "So does it depend wholly on our grammar what will be called (logically) possible and what not ...." (*Philosophical Investigations*, p. 142e).

[2] *F.u.t.L.*, p. 20.

[3] J. P. Sartre emphasizes this. Compare his "The Journey and the Return" which is a critical essay on Brice Parain's, *Recherches sur la nature et les fonctions du langage*, Paris, 1942. Sartre's essay is included in *Essays on Language and Literature*, edited by J. L. Heveni, London, Allen Wingate.

the noematic aspect may always be viewed as having been
constituted in the noetic aspect, here also in our experience of
language there is a noetic experience which produces the identity
of the word, a meaning-intending act which produces the identity
of meaning, and an act which constitutes the two, the physical
expression and the meaning, into an inseparable unity. The
underlying insight seems to be that man, as an animal possessed
of speech, is not a passive witness of an objective structure
which exists independent of him; nor is he a mechanic who uses
ready-made tools. But, a spiritual being as he is, his experience is
creative; he produces language and uses it. The objectivity of
linguistic expression is rooted in the subjective acts of the
speaker.

(b) The development of Husserl's philosophy in general from
the *Ideen* Vol. I onwards is marked by an increasing awareness of
the importance of the *Lebenswelt*, an awareness that brings him
nearer Dewey and Whitehead in one major aspect.[1] The ideality
and the objectivity of expressions and thought-structures are
not for a moment lost sight of. Nor is the doctrine of the noetic
constituting acts given up. Only, the transition to the noetic acts
is now sought to be *mediated by* one more step: the demonstration
that all those objectivities and their experiences derive from one
unreflective *Lebenswelt*. The transcendental idealism expands its
fold so as to include even the unreflective primitive order of life
within its scope, instead of leaving it untouched as an irrational
Other. (Kantian idealism, Husserl tells us in his *Krisis*,[2] did not
see this presupposition of all thought and of all science.)

The general principle regarding the relation of the idealities
to the *Lebenswelt* is laid down thus in *Die Krisis:* "...objective
theory in its logical sense... is rooted in the *Lebenswelt*, in the
original evidences belonging to it. By virtue of this foundation,
objective science acquires a standing significance for the world
in which we always live even as scientists and, then also as the
community of co-scientists – that is to say for the common
Lebenswelt." [3] And yet, the structure raised on this foundation is
something new.[4]

[1] See the concluding chapter of this work.
[2] *Krisis*, § 28.
[3] *Krisis*, p. 132.
[4] *ibid.*, p. 133.

For philosophy of language, the transition to the *Lebenswelt* means the transition from *language to speech*, to interpersonal communication. "The environment (*Umwelt*) which constitutes itself in the experience of the Other, in reciprocal understanding and in agreement is called by us the *communicative* environment."[1] In this environment, speech is followed by reply, suggestions are followed by assent or dissent or even a counterproposal. Within this environment, persons enter into relationship with other persons. A person speaks to another.[2] The *I* is relative to the *we*. The *I* requires a *you*, and the *we* requires the *others*.[3] It is out of this interpersonal situation that language as an objectified structure arises.[4]

It would be interesting to compare these two aspects of Husserl's philosophy of language with a similar distinction made by Saussure between a "synchronic" linguistic of speech and a "diachronic" linguistic of language, or with Pos's distinction between the phenomenological and the objective attitudes. The objective attitude, according to Pos, looks at language in the past tense; this is the attitude of the observer who surveys the history of language, who regards a language as a product of past acts of signification, of past hazards and accidents. In short, in this attitude we seek for the historical origin and growth of language and look upon the present as a resultant of this process. The phenomenological attitude, on the other hand, returns to the speaking subject, to the "communicative" *Umwelt* as Husserl calls it, or to the speech as "coming warm from the human mouth" as Sartre [5] puts it.

How are we to place Husserl in such a context? It must at once be obvious that Husserl in no phase of his philosophy had anything to do with the objective attitude in the sense explained above, for his phenomenological method could not possibly have had anything to do with the historical origin and growth of

---

[1] *Ideen* II (*Husserliana*, Bd. IV), p. 193.

[2] *ibid.*, p. 236.

[3] *ibid.*, p. 288, footnote.

[4] Compare Brice Parain: "I am hungry. It is I who am saying: I am hungry; but it is not me who is understood. I have disappeared in these two seconds whilst I am speaking. As soon as I have spoken, there remains no more of me than a man who is hungry, and this man is common to everyone ... I am transformed into an impersonal order." *Recherches sur la nature et les fonctions du langage*, p. 172, quoted by J. P. Sartre, *loc. cit.*, p. 184-5.

[5] J. P. Sartre, *loc. cit.*

language. Both his earlier *eidetic* phase and the later *constitutive* phase including the return to the *Lebenswelt* fall within the legitimate phenomenological attitude. In fact, one could even maintain that the eidetic phase, especially the doctrine of the *Idealität des Sprachlichen*, could have been developed only from the phenomenological attitude of the communicating subject, for it is only when regarded from the situation of inter-subjective communication that a linguistic expression proclaims its ideality. Thus one could venture the seemingly paradoxical assertion that the phenomenological attitude reveals at once the subjectivity and the objectivity, the relativity and the absoluteness of linguistic expressions.[1],[2]

13.3.   With this account of the Husserlian philosophy of language in mind, we might now turn to the contemporary philosophical scene for finding out the relevance of Husserl's thoughts. Contemporary philosophical attitudes towards language might be brought under three broad headings, each head admittedly permitting a large degree of internal variation. These three attitudes may be termed: (*a*) Positivism (*b*) Existentialism and (*c*) Neo-Humboldtian metalinguistics. A few words about each would serve our purpose.[3]

(*a*) *Positivism* – Today one hardly needs to be reminded that 'logical Positivism' is a title that is applied to a large number of diverse trends of thought. After the early enthusiasm over the verifiability theory of meaning has nearly died out, there remains hardly any philosopher who would call himself a logical positivist without qualification. Today one can only use that name to stand for two totally different attitudes, agreeing only in one negative point: the therapeutic motive connected with a distrust of metaphysics. The one i.e. the school of later Wittgen-

[1] It is interesting to compare the development of Husserl's philosophy with the development of Ernst Cassirer's philosophy of language. Cassirer started with a genetic view of language and gradually abandoned it in favour of a phenomenological philosophy. cp. Lenneberg, "A note on Cassirer's Philosophy of Language," *Philosophical and Phenomenological Research*, Vol. XV, pp. 512–522.

[2] Compare Parain: Language is "neither subject nor object, is pertaining neither to one nor the other, subject whilst I am speaking, object whilst I hear myself speaking ...." (*Recherches sur la nature et les fonctions du langage*, p. 183; quoted *loc. cit.*, p. 180).

[3] In the rest of this section I have made extensive use of an earlier published paper of mine, "Types of Linguistic Philosophy," *The Viswabharati Quarterly*, Vol. 25, No. 2.

stein is primarily concerned with ordinary use of language; the other, ably represented in the U.S.A., distrusts ordinary language and is concerned with the construction of artificial, logically perfect languages.

(i) The contemporary distrust of ordinary language has its origin in the logician's ideal of perfection. Two motives may be singled out for the present: first, it is held that in ordinary language the grammatical form of sentences conceals rather than show their logical form. This leads, as is well known, to metaphysical muddles. In an ideal language, the logical form of sentences can be directly seen, without taking recourse to further logical manoeuvres. This, the formalists hope, would serve the above-mentioned therapeutic motive better. Secondly, usages permitted within ordinary language give rise to paradoxes and self-contradictions; it is only an artificially constructed logically perfect language that could be free from such paradoxes.

(ii) We shall refer, not to the truth-functional view of language of the *Tractatus*, but to the philosophy of language of the *Philosophical Investigations*. To the formalist's censure of ordinary language, Wittgenstein replies thus: "The more narrowly we examine actual language, the sharper becomes the conflict between it and our requirement. (For the crystalline purity of logic was, of course, not a *result of investigation:* it was a requirement).[1] There is "no *single* ideal of exactness," "unless you yourself lay down what is to be so called." [2] Further, "It is *primarily* the apparatus of our ordinary language, of our word–language, that we call language; and then other things by analogy or comparability with this." [3]

There is no one feature belonging in common to all that we call language. "Instead of producing something common to all that we call language, I am saying that these phenomena have no one thing in common which makes us use the same word for all, – but that they are *related* to one another in many different ways. And it is because of this relationship, or these relationships, that we call them all "language." [4] Just as the different games are games not by virtue of a common property possessed by them

[1] *Philosophical Investigations*, p. 46e.
[2] *ibid.*, p. 42e.
[3] *ibid.*, p. 138e.
[4] *ibid.*, p. 31e.

all but because of a "family resemblance," so are different languages languages because of "families of structures more or less related to one another." [1] Each language is a game with its own immanent rules. There are alternative language-games. Mastering a language is like mastering a game, knowing how to play it according to its rules.

This immanent view of language leads Wittgenstein to reject radically any reference of language to something non-linguistic, be it things, concepts or mental states. "The question is not one of explaining a language-game by means of our experiences, but of noting a language-game." "Look on the language-game as the *primary* thing. And look on the feelings, etc., as you look on a way of regarding the language-game, as interpretation." [2] Even ostensive definition does not provide us with a way out of the language-game, for even ostensive definition presupposes the language-game: "the ostensive definition explains the use – the meaning–of the word when the overall role of the word in language is clear." [3] Just as language does not presuppose ostensive definition, so it does not also express thoughts. To think is to play a language-game.

Now, since a language is a game, and since no move in a game can have any sense when isolated from the entire game, it should follow that no word or expression of a language has a meaning as isolated from the context of the entire system of language. As Ryle has insisted, the old distinction between categorematic and syncategorematic expressions has to be abandoned, all expressions being syncategorematic. The language-game, Wittgenstein says, is the "original home" of the word.[4]

Lastly, a language-game is not an arbitrary and fanciful luxury, but is a *"Lebensform,"* a form of life. It is this insight which presumably is responsible, at least in part, for Wittgenstein's refusal to indulge in fanciful constructions of artificial languages. The task of philosophy is to accept, to take note of, and to describe the given and not to reform it.

But, Wittgenstein is not altogether free from the therapeutic motive: "philosophical problems arise where language *goes on*

---

[1] *ibid.*, p. 46e.
[2] *ibid.*, p. 167e.
[3] *ibid.*, p. 14e.
[4] *ibid.*, p. 48e.

holiday.'' [1] Complete clarity about the rules of language simply
means that the philosophical problems should totally disappear.[2]

(*b*) *Existentialism* – The Existentialist philosophers do not lag
behind any others in their interest in language. But their formulation of the philosophical problem of language is singularly
unlike that of the others. What is the significance of language,
they ask, so far as human existence is concerned? To this
question the different existentialist philosophers no doubt offer
different answers. But they all seem to agree in drawing a distinction between *authentic* language and *inauthentic* language,
the former being more intimately related to the essential characters of human existence than the latter. According to Heidegger,
the doyen of the German existentialists (and one who stands
nearest to Husserl in many ways), language is not merely a
concrete tool for expressing thoughts that need communication.
Nor is language merely the meaning of those expressions. That
language is expression and has meaning is not denied. But none
of these characteristics reveals to us the *essence* of language.
The essential function of language, according to Heidegger, is to
manifest Being (and therefore also the beings) to man.[3] Where
there is no language, there is no awareness of being. The origin
of language, shrouded in mystery as it is, coincides with the
opening up of Being for man. It coincides therefore with human
existence itself, for human existence consists, in its innermost
core, in awareness of Being.[4] Man may be characterized as the
animal having language, an improvement over, or perhaps an
explication of, Cassirer's characterization of man as symbol-
using animal. Man does not use language because he thinks; he
thinks because he has language. Man pretends as if he were architect
or the master of language, whereas in fact language is his master.[5]
In authentic language, Heidegger says, Being itself speaks: the
nearest approach to it being the inspired language of poetry. In

---

[1] *ibid.*, p. 19e.
[2] *ibid.*, p. 51e.
[3] Language in its beginning was the "Being become articulate" (*Wortwerden des Seins*): See M. Heidegger, *Einführung in die Metaphysik*, Tübingen, 1953, p. 131. In his letter *Über den Humanismus*, Bern, 2nd ed., 1954, Heidegger writes at the end that language is the language of Being.
[4] Hans Lipps, Husserl's Schüler and one who represented a very early link between phenomenology and existentialism poses the same problem in his *Untersuchungen zu einer hermeneutischen Logik*, Frankfurt, 1938.
[5] M. Heidegger, *Vorträge und Aufsätze*, Pfullingen, 1954, p. 190.

its inauthentic mode, language degenerates into 'talk' (*Gerede*).
In the former case, we *speak* in the true sense; in the latter case,
we *make use of* language as we make use of a tool.[1] The more
authenticity one's language does achieve, the more truly does
one exist. Degradation of existence and degeneration of language
go together.

Another existentialist thinker, Martin Buber seeks to distinguish between the way man communicates to man and the
way animals communicate amongst themselves.[2] First, although
calling or appealing to another (*Anrufen*) is to be found also in
other animals, it is man alone who *addresses himself* to another
(*Anreden*). And such addressing oneself to another is based
upon a recognition of the independence of the Other. Secondly, man not only speaks but also sets up and posits what he
speaks as an independent object, as something finished and
self-subsisting. Through this process, the *Anrede* neutralizes
itself;[3] but it always has the possibility of becoming 'living' in
genuine dialogue.

Two points are worth noticing. Buber recognizes two aspects
of language: the living dialogue and the objective expression.
The logician does justice only to the second of the two. According to Buber, the latter arises out of, and again passes into
the former. Further, like Heidegger, Buber also distinguishes
between genuine dialogue and spurious conversation; the former
is based upon an acceptance of the Other,[4] through which the
persons communicating are guaranteed of their own individuali-
ties.

(c) *Humboldt* – It should not be supposed that by postponing
this mention of Humboldtian attitude towards language to the
last, we want to underestimate its importance. Historically,
Humboldt ranks first. But what is more than this is, that
Humboldt's may be regarded as one of the first attempts to
study language philosophically.[5] If therefore he is mentioned
after Logical Positivism and Existentialism, it could only be
due to the fact that these two latter schools are engaging con-

---

[1] M. Heidegger, *Was heisst Denken?* Tübingen, 1954, p. 87.
[2] M. Buber, *Urdistanz und Beziehung*, Heidelberg, 1951, p. 34 f.
[3] Compare Parain, quoted in footnote 2 on page 66 above.
[4] M. Buber, *loc. cit.*, p. 36.
[5] W. v. Humboldt, *Uber die Verschiedenheit des menschlichen Sprachbaues*, 1836.

temporary philosophical attention as no other school does.

Humboldt's philosophy of language has two aspects, the static and the dynamic, the objective and the subjective. The objective aspect of his philosophy of language consists in three beliefs: the idea of a perfect language towards which all empirical languages are approximations; the idea that each language, notwithstanding all its endless specialities, variations and niceties, has *an inner form* which again conceals a certain metaphysical world-view; and finally, the notion that language does not owe its being merely to its use by men but has a peculiar existence of its own.

In its dynamic aspect, his philosophy of language goes back from the conception of language as a finished product (*Werk*, Ergon) to the conception of it as an activity (*Tätigkeit*, Energeia).[1] Language is now no more a dead product but a living production.[2] In its real nature, it is always transcending itself, always incomplete, perpetually being produced in living communication.[3]

And yet these two aspects enter into an inalienable unity in Humboldt's thought.[4] Humboldt himself does not fail to notice this unity. Language is both objective and subjective, both independent and dependent.[5]

The neo-Humboldtians have developed in different directions. Whorf substantiates Humboldt's thesis that every language has a hidden metaphysic by an astonishing fulness of data collected by careful study of many different languages. Lipps – who, it may be said, provides a link between Humboldt and Husserl – develops a remarkable thesis about the relational nature of language.[6] The real language consists, according to Lipps, not in the abstract form which logic and science impart to it but in the living conversation that takes place between persons and persons. Looking at language from this point of

---

[1] *ibid.*, p. 44.

[2] *ibid.*, p. 43.

[3] *ibid.*, p. 44–5.

[4] B. Croce wrongly takes this to be an inner contradiction in Humboldt. See his *Aesthetics*, London, 1909, pp. 318–9.

[5] "*Die beiden hier angeregten, einander entgegengesetzten Ansichten, dass die Sprache der Seele fremd und ihr angehörend, von ihr unabhängig und abhängig ist, verbinden sich wirklich in ihr und machen die Eigentümlichkeit ihres Wesens aus .... Die Sprache ist gerade insofern objektiv einwirkend und selbständig, als sie subjektiv gewirkt und abhängig ist.*" (*loc. cit.*, p. 64).

[6] H. Lipps, *loc. cit.*

view, Lipps rejects all those philosophies that consider language in its relation to something extra-linguistic. It is usual to treat words either as expressions of inner thought processes or as names of external objects, or even as standing for ideal meaning-unities. Lipps rejects all such approaches. The matter of fact (or *sachliche*) meanings of expressions are based upon their original and *linguistic* (or *sprachliche*) meanings. The *linguistic* meaning of an expression only indicates the *direction* in which it by virtue of its linguistic roots points. What, for example, Lipps asks in the manner of Wittgenstein, is the meaning of 'playing'? None of the real instances is merely playing, none is wholly playing! The real meaning of 'playing' can only be progressively realized, that is to say concretized, by running through its endless concrete manifestations. The linguistic meaning gives only a possibility, a direction, a form. The meaning of words cannot therefore bestated in a ready-made fashion. It can only be laid bare progressively through examples. (Ryle and Wittgenstein are perhaps, in one sense, doing this)

13.4.   It is needless to emphasize that the interest in language is a healthy sign of a new era in man's attempt to understand himself. But amidst these diverse attitudes towards language, it is necessary to determine in *which direction* a truly satisfactory philosophy of language should develop. If this were possible, we would have gained the perspective for a proper appreciation of Husserl, which of course is the immediate task before us. For this purpose, the following remarks may here be made:

(*a*) At the outset we must guard ourselves against the temptation to let the therapeutic motive dominate our philosophizing about language. For the interest in curing metaphysical evils is born out of a hidden metaphysical obsession; with most modern positivists it is the obsession with sensationalism and phenomenalism. A satisfactory philosophy of language should be, at least in its starting point, free from such metaphysical prejudices. Its task, as Wittgenstein rightly saw, is not to justify anything, but to describe what is given.

(*b*) The construction of artificial languages is therefore devoid of any *major* philosophical importance. These languages are parts of formal logic understood in a wide sense, and they contribute neither towards a philosophic understanding of ordinary language nor towards a solution or dissolution of other philosophical problems. In fact, the so-called ideal, or logically perfect languages are not languages at all. A choice from amongst them does not amount – to use Wittgenstein's phrase – to the choice of a *Lebensform*. They lack, we could say, the inevitability and the overwhelming character which belong to languages strictly so-called.

(c) It is for this last reason that Wittgenstein's idea of language-game seems highly misleading. In spite of his recognition that a language represents a *Lebensform*, in spite of his rejection of all artificial languages and his decision merely to describe what is given, and further in spite of his distrust of mere possibilities, Wittgenstein yet indulges in the fanciful construction of alternate language-games which correspond to no actual language, and therefore, strictly speaking, are artificial, if not formal. Wittgenstein, in spite of his rare insight, was making too much of a piece of clear but misleading hit.

(d) Both the formalists and the existentialists distinguish between ordinary language and ideal language. But the criteria and the nature of the ideal language are different in the two cases. The formalist's ideal language is impersonal, free from all content (even what are called "the undefined descriptive predicates" are to be replaced by symbols) and the criterion is logical consistency. His criticism of ordinary language is that the latter is not logical enough. The existentialist's ideal language is deeply personal, for it must issue out of intimate and personal self-awareness and not out of the impersonal knowledge or opinion of common sense and science. The existentialist however *cannot* make a radical break with ordinary language, for does not he hold the view that *all* language is of existential significance? His ideal language can never mean a complete departure from ordinary language. In this respect, he is right.

(e) Again, whereas the formalist, finding that ordinary language is not *logical* enough, seeks refuge in artificial ones, Husserl finds the logical in the nature of all language, i.e. in the nature of expression as such. For the logical, according to

Husserl, concerns also the content, and not merely the form. All expressions exhibit a real, transitory, and an ideal abiding aspect.

(f) At this point, the existentialists join issue; so also do Wittgenstein, Ryle and Hans Lipps. Language, they would point out as against Husserl, is not a finished product, separable from the context of speaking, addressing etc. Living language belongs to the actual relational situation consisting, amongst other factors, of a speaker and a hearer. Husserl's idealized, hypostatized linguistic expression is but the product of anatomical dissection of a living process. The physiology of a living organism is not there.

A satisfactory philosophy of language must recognize both these aspects. Such is the nature of language that it at once arises out of a real, concrete, and personal situation and yet assumes the status of an ideal, abstract, and impersonal expression. To try to account for this, i.e. to show *how* this could be so would be a risky venture; for one is apt to make use of one's concealed metaphysical preconceptions. We could only recognize that it *is* so and describe it. Buber, of all the thinkers we have mentioned, describes the situation most accurately. Man addresses himself to another; but he also separates himself (*"distanziert sich"*) from his utterances, by virtue of which act language exhibits its ideal character. Existentialists err when they think that true communication is incurably personal; Wittgensteinians err when they treat it as wholly relational. All communication is personal-impersonal, real-ideal, concrete-abstract.

This corroborates what we said before (§ 13.2.): "Thus one could venture the seemingly paradoxical assertion that the phenomenological attitude reveals at once the subjectivity and the objectivity, the relativity and the absoluteness of linguistic expressions."

§ 14.   We are now in a better position than before to appreciate the exact nature of Husserl's Platonism. Husserl is far from indulging in a naive ontology. He is concerned *not* with the existence of entities,[1] but with the intentional correlates of

---

[1] This in fact is one of the objections raised against Husserl by his ontologically oriented followers, e.g. by Nicolai Hartmann.

meaning-intending experiences. Phenomenology is not to go beyond the given. The object *as given* that is to say – in the widest sense of givenness – *as intended*, is the final resting place for objectively oriented phenomenology: *this does not as such amount to ontology*. The object as intended is the Noema; the act of intending is the Noesis. The ideality of the noema has to be placed in the context of that noematic-noetic correlation which is the central theme of Husserl's later philosophy. Looked at from one point of view, the noema or the intentional correlate dissolves into the subjective experiences, the mere intentions, of which it represents a limiting end. From another point of view, the noetic acts reveal themselves as merely leading up to the intended object whose autonomy however they do not affect.[1] Both descriptions are correct. They make up for each other's one-sidedness and together build the true perspective for a phenomenological philosophy.

An analogy from quite another field would perhaps serve to illuminate the situation. In physics, it has come to be recognized that both the wave theory and the corpuscular theory of light, in general of elementary particles, are admissible alternative descriptions of the phenomena concerned. The two theories are not now, as they were before, regarded as conflicting hypotheses. We owe it to the insight of modern physics that they are now looked upon as complementary descriptions. We could perhaps similarly say that we owe it to the insight of phenomenology that Platonic idealization and subjectivistic relativization are not conflicting but complementary descriptions of phenomena that could only be described in such *alternations*.

14.1. At the end of this chapter, let us examine in brief two usual charges brought against Platonism in the theory of meaning and ask, if they affect a theory like that of Husserl.

In the first place, Ryle's 'Fido'-Fido principle [2] deserves our attention. Ryle is, in effect, drawing our attention to the mis-

---

[1] cp. "... *diese ursprünglich erwerbende Aktivität ist die "Evidenz" für diese Idealitäten. Evidenz, ganz allgemein, ist eben nichts anderes als die Bewusstseinsweise, die eventl.... ihre intentionale Gegenständlichkeit im Modus des originalen "es selbst" darbietet.* (F.u.t.L., p. 150). It is to be noted that Husserl equates "*erzeugen*" with "*darbieten*," paradoxical though this might appear.

[2] G. Ryle, "The Theory of Meaning," *British Philosophy in Mid-century*, ed. by Mace); and Ryle, "Meaning and Necessity," *Philosophy*, 1949.

leading equation of signifying with naming, as a consequence of which philosophers – not all of whom are Platonists – have come to treat all meaningful expressions as names. Although philosophers other than the Platonists are guilty of this mistake, it is the Platonists who deserve special attention, for it is in their case that the absurdity of treating all words as names can be seen most clearly. Quine in the same vein traces Platonism to a failure to distinguish between meaning and reference. In reply, it can be said that the diagnosis is not correct. Frege and Husserl did distinguish between meaning and reference, and it is unlikely that after having drawn the distinction they should have so soon flouted it. Further, we have said that the exclusion of all question about reference leaves us in a better position to be able to appreciate Platonism. Platonism cannot be eliminated in this way. It can only be balanced by an emphasis upon the other aspect of the meaning-situation to which attention has been drawn in the above section. Husserl, of all persons, never succumbed to the 'Fido'-Fido principle in the sense of equating signifying with denoting. Not only does he avoid this equation; he even sees that 'referring' does not always amount to 'naming.'

In the second place, it has been pointed out that Platonism in theory of meaning involves the absurd thesis that when we understand an expression or meaningfully use one, we are inspecting some curious entities called meanings. It is however clear by now that this objection hardly does justice to Husserl. For he is clearly aware that in meaning-intending experience we are not objectively aware of the meaning itself. To have an experience and to apprehend the intentional correlate of that experience *objectively* are quite different things. It is only in a subsequent act of reflection that we could be said to be objectively aware of the meaning.[2]

[1] See § 6.2. above.
[2] See § 9.2. above.

CHAPTER V

CERTAIN ASSOCIATED PROBLEMS

A. ON 'OCCASIONAL EXPRESSIONS'

§ 15. It has been pointed out in § 12.1. that the ambiguities and fluctuations in meaning could be eliminated, for these pertain not to the meanings themselves but to our use of a seemingly identical physical expression. This explanation of the phenomena of ambiguity and fluctuation, howsoever plausible it may be in the case of expressions like 'water,' 'table,' 'hand,' has much lesser chance of succeeding in the case of the so-called 'occasional' expressions (or, 'indexical' expressions or 'ego-centric particulars') like 'I' and 'this.' Is it possible even in such cases to demonstrate the ideality of meaning amidst the change of persons and situations? Is the subjectivity and the equivocation attached to such expressions a dispensable accident? Is it possible, that is to say, to eliminate their ego-centricity? To find out Husserl's answer to such questions, we should follow him in his analysis of the so-called occasional expressions.[1]

The analysis starts with a distinction between 'objective' expressions and 'subjective' expressions. An expression is objective, if it is possible to fix its meaning through its mere sound-sensory appearance. It follows that such an expression is intelligible without necessarily referring to the person using it or the circumstances under which it is used. It is quite possible that an objective expression is equivocal; in that case it is related to many different meanings in the same relationship, so that a reference to the circumstances of its use would be necessary in order to determine which of the meanings it carries in a particular case. But whether the expression at all can be understood in any of those meanings is *not* dependent on such circumstances of its

[1] Compare *L.U.*, II, 1, pp. 79–90; *L.U.*, II, 2, pp. 18–23.

use as its *conditio sine qua non*. The equivocation of objective
expressions does not therefore destroy the theory of the ideality
of meanings.

An expression is subjective and 'occasional' if it owns "a
conceptually unitary group of possible meanings" in such a
manner that its *actual* meaning in any particular case is *essentially dependent* on the person using it and the circumstances
of its use. Such, e.g., are the expressions 'I', 'this', 'here' etc.

Husserl's analysis of such expressions is not without origi-
nality. The first point to be borne in mind is that the expression
'I' is not entirely meaningless even when the person using
it and the circumstances of its use are unknown; even in such
a case the word 'I' is different from 'Abracadabra.' We know
that the word refers to the person speaking and that the person
speaking calls himself by this name. But, on the other hand, it
is equally clear that this does not constitute the full meaning of
the expression 'I,' for, if it were so, then in every statement
containing 'I,' the 'I' could be replaced by 'the person speaking
at the moment' without any loss of meaning for the statement.
This, however, is not the case, as can easily be shown. We have,
therefore, to distinguish between two components, i.e., two
layers as it were of the full meaning of 'I': one, its general
meaning-function and the other, that which determines this
general function and transforms it into the full, real and concrete
meaning. Husserl calls the former the 'signifying' meaning
(*anzeigende Bedeutung*) and the latter the 'signified' meaning
(*angezeigte Bedeutung*). Similarly with the 'this' and the 'here':
we have on the one hand a general function of pointing out, and
on the other, as if built upon the first, the full determinate
meaning. So far as the former is concerned, one could say that
even the occasional expressions retain an identical unvarying
component amidst their shifting and changing meanings. Even
in the case of the 'this,' [1] perception makes the meaning definite
but does not constitute it; it is to be regarded *als Bedeutung
bestimmende* but not *als Bedeutung enthaltende*.

It follows from this analysis that the 'this' and the 'I' are
semi-conceptual; as general, their meanings are not wholly
determinate and receive their full determinations only from

---

[1] *L.U.*, II, 2, p. 19–20.

extraneous circumstances.[1] Because of their semi-conceptual character, Husserl refuses to treat them as 'logically proper names' in the manner of Russell. Of course, 'this,' like proper names, directly names its object; and as in the case of proper names, so also here the meaning receives its full determination from perception. But nevertheless there are important differences.[2] In the first place, the 'this' with its semi-conceptual meaning-function of 'pointing towards' introduces an element of mediacy which is not present in the relation of proper names to their objects. In the second place, the proper name always belongs to its object, whereas the 'this' has not this fixity.[3] It is obvious that the 'I' requires a different account.

Are the occasional expressions eliminable? For Russell this question means: are the egocentric particulars necessary for a complete description of the world? For Husserl, the question is: is the subjectivity and the changing character of the meanings of these expressions consistent with that identity and fixity of meaning which a phenomenology of thought demands? Both, in reply, consider the egocentricity and the shifting character of these expressions dispensable.

Already in its use in mathematical-scientific discourse, Husserl argues, the demonstrative has got rid of its subjectivity.[4] Generally speaking, according to Husserl, every subjective expression can be replaced with an objective one if only we could get hold of its momentary meaning-intention in its identity.[5] Also for

---

[1] Russell also recognizes this: "There is obviously a general concept involved, namely, 'object of attention,' but something more than this general concept is required in order to secure the temporary uniqueness of 'this'." (*Inquiry into Meaning and Truth*, London, 1940, p. 111).

[2] *L.U.*, II, 2, p. 20–1.

[3] Russell also recognizes two points of difference between 'this' and proper names. First, 'this' is not like the name 'Smith,' which applies to many objects, but to each always; the name 'this' applies to only one object at a time, and when it begins to apply to a new object it ceases to be applicable to the old one" (*loc. cit.*, p. 109). Secondly, "If I say that 'this' is a name, I am left with the problem of explaining on what principle we decide what it names on different occasions." (*loc. cit.*, p. 110). The different Smiths do not have in common any property of smithyness; but we do *not* call a thing 'this' simply by arbitrary convention.

[4] Russell asks: Can two persons experience the same 'this'? and answers: "... two people are more likely to have the same 'this' if it is somewhat abstract than if it is fully concrete. In fact, broadly speaking, every increase of abstractness diminishes the difference between one person's world and another's" (*Human Knowledge, Its Scope and Limits*, London, 1948, p. 108).

[5] *L.U.*, II, 1, p. 90.

Russell, the 'this' can always be replaced by the name 'W' which would be the name for a bundle of qualities.[1]

It must be said that Husserl's attempt to eliminate egocentric particulars from language is as much defective, and fails precisely for the same reasons as Russell's 'particular-free' analysis.[2]

Husserl's attempt to eliminate the egocentric particulars also corresponds to his own search, in the *Ideen*,[3] for *an essence* of the 'this-there.' He speaks there of "an individual fact's own essence" (which, it must be noted, is not the same as an "individual essence"). But he does not seem to have realized the impossibility of absorbing the uniqueness of the *this-now* into, or of deducing the same from, an essence, however articulated and structured that essence may be. The 'this' is a category of the real world, and not of the realm of essences – to use the *language of naive ontology. The phenomenological discontinuity* between them and the ideal-objective meanings has to be recognized. This discontinuity sets a limit to all deductive metaphysics. It is also a discontinuity between the corresponding modes of givenness, to speak in the *phenomenological mode*. Speaking in the *formal mode*, it is the distinction between two groups of expressions that resist assimilation to a common mould. Here then is a limit to the theory of the ideality of meanings. True Platonism is dualistic, it recognizes a dualism between particulars and universals. In theory of meaning, it has to recognize a distinction between those that are capable of idealization and those that resist such idealization, or let us suggest, between the theoretical and the practical expressions.[4]

B. ON NON-EXTENSIONAL EXPRESSIONS

§ 16.   The theory of meaning developed in the foregoing pages suffers from another limitation. Contemporary philosophers have very aptly drawn attention to the "enormously many uses of language other than that of making statements."[5]

---

[1] Russell, *Inquiry*, p. 128.

[2] For a criticism of Russell's 'particular-free' analysis, see G. Bergmann, *Metaphysics of Logical Positivism*, Longmans Green, 1954, pp. 197–214.

[3] *Ideen*, p. 35.

[4] P. F. Strawson's "Singular Terms, Ontology and Identity," *Mind*, 1956, 433–454, offers a forceful argument against the opposite tendency.

[5] G. J. Warnock, *English Philosophy since 1900*, Oxford, 1958, p. 129.

"We use words," in the words of Warnock, "to give orders, ask questions, express wishes, pass verdicts, to pray and to swear and to give undertakings." [1] Now the theory of meaning developed in the foregoing pages, if at all it holds good, is valid only of (i) isolated words or phrases (excepting the egocentric particulars and expressions containing such particulars) and (ii) of sentences used to make statements. But does it hold good of sentences expressing wishes, verdicts, promises, and questions?

The distinction, however, is not unknown to Husserl who, as we have said before in § 10.1., distinguishes between objectifying and not-objectifying intentional acts. In the concluding section of the *Logische Untersuchungen*, Husserl undertakes the task of enquiring into the nature of the expressions expressing such not-objectifying acts as desire, question, hope, order etc. Do these acts also *carry* meaning? That is how the issue has been stated in an earlier context.[2]

One cannot say with full justification that the distinction between statement-making sentences and sentences used to express wishes, pass orders or ask questions was unknown to Aristotle and the later logicians. One can of course very well feel dissatisfied with the way they interpreted the latter group of sentences.

Husserl asks: "Are the well-known grammatical forms which language has... coined... for wishes, questions and desires – generally speaking, for acts not belonging to the class of objectifying ones – to be looked upon as *judgments over* these acts or can these acts themselves – and not merely the objectifying ones – function as the 'expressed' acts, that is to say, as meaning-conferring and meaning-fulfilling." [3] Or, in other words, wherein lie the *meanings* of sentences expressing wishes or asking questions or passing orders? Two answers seem to be possible: either the meaning of such a sentence lies *in the act it expresses*, a wish, a question or an order; or the meaning lies *in some judgment (about* that act i.e., the wish, the question, or the order) implicit in the sentence. There is no doubt that formulated in this manner the issue is not at once clear, as it presupposes the

[1] *ibid.*, p. 129.
[2] *L.U.*, II, 2, § 1, p. 8. The question that is asked is: "*Ob alle oder nur gewisse Akt-arten als Bedeutungsträger fungieren können*"?
[3] *L.U.*, II, 2, p. 207.

many fine distinctions Husserl has drawn between several possible meanings of 'expressing.' But, put in more familiar words, the issue seems to be this: are sentences asking questions or expressing wishes or passing orders *as such* meaningful, or are they meaningful only as implicitly containing a statement, an assertion of some sort?

Husserl is placed in an embarrassing situation, for he has to take into account two facts both of which he finds acceptable: on the one hand he recognizes that there is a *radical difference* between these sentences and sentences making statements. In Husserl's manner of speaking, they are not merely different sorts of sentences, but are, *as sentences*, different. On the other hand, he holds that it is only the so-called objectifying acts that could function as *bearer* of meaning, so that since wishes, questions, orders etc. are not objectifying acts they could not as such, i.e., merely as wishes, questions, orders etc. function as meaning-intending. He has thus to steer clear of two extreme views. There is on the one hand the Aristotelian theory that sentences expressing wishes, asking questions or passing orders not only are irreducible to statements but also do not contain any statement. For, a statement is that which can be true or false, whereas a question, a wish or an imperative cannot be true or false. And yet wish-sentences, questions or imperatives are all meaningful, not by virtue of any statement they are making (for they are not making any) but precisely by virtue of those intentional experiences i.e. the wish, the question, the order, which they are expressing. Names express representations; statements express judgments; wish-sentences express wishes; and so on. Each of these acts – be it objectifying or non-objectifying–can 'carry' meaning, i.e. can, *as such*, function as meaning-intending.

On the other hand, there is an opposite point of view according to which wish-sentences, questions or orders certainly do contain statements. A question, e.g., may be said to state that the person who is asking seeks to get the proper information. The question 'Is S P?' would in that case be equivalent to the statement 'I ask if S is P.' The statement is about the 'announced'[1] experience of the speaker. Any one who speaks is thereby announcing something; there must therefore be a corresponding statement.

[1] About the *announcing* function of expressions, see § 4 above.

Before proceeding further it should be noted that although the Aristotelian view seeks to emphasize the distinction between sentences making statements and sentences used for other purposes by refusing to reduce the latter to the former, yet it also in a way treats them alike in so far as it holds that a wish, a question or an order is, as such, as much a meaning-intending experience as a judgment is. Husserl would not permit this manner of obliterating the distinction. A non-objectifying act as such could *not* possibly, according to Husserl, function as meaning-intending. Hence in so far as sentences of this group possess theoretical meaning there must be objectifying experiences (or corresponding statements) underlying them. But in that case where are we to find the objectifying act, i.e. the judgment which as it were lends theoretical meaning to a sentence of this group?

16.1. Let us consider the answer that immediately suggests itself. The question 'Is S P?', it may be said, is equivalent to the *statement* 'I ask if S is P,' the latter being a statement of, or a judgment about the experience of the questioner which is the same as the announced (*kundgegeben*) experience.

To this it might be replied that if this equivalence holds good, then it should likewise hold good that the *statement* 'S is P' is equivalent to the statement 'I judge that S is P.' But this would land us in an infinite regress, for this latter statement would be, on the same ground, equivalent to 'I judge that I judge that S is P.' It might further be replied that the reference to the questioner is not contained in the meaning of a question *qua* question. In communicative speech, no doubt, the person spoken to apprehends the speaker *as* one who is asking (or judging or wishing, as the case may be). But this effect of communicative speech cannot be taken as constituting the meaning of the expression. For the same expression also functions meaningfully in lonely speech.[1] Now, taken outside of communicative function, the reference to the questioner is not an essential component of a question: hence the above equivalence does not do justice to a question as a question.

---

[1] For Husserl's distinction between lonely speech and communicative speech, see § 5 above.

The above arguments against the proposed reduction of 'Is S P?' to 'I ask if S is P' prove only this much that the meaning in all types of sentences is not constituted by a component that is essentially related to the communicative function. Every sentence that is uttered cannot therefore be interpreted as a judgment over (or as a statement of)the 'announced' inner experience of the speaker. But from this it does *not* follow that the sentences under consideration are not judgments over the relevant experiences (questions, wishes etc.). It is, on the other hand, quite possible that only in so far as they *are* such judgments that they are capable of adequately 'expressing' those experiences. The judgments they might in this sense contain need not be predicative judgments, but could very well be judgments in the wider sense of "positing objectification." [1]

To the argument that the proposed equivalence should also apply to statement-making sentences (and would then lead to an infinite regress), it may be replied by saying that the situation with regard to statement-making sentences is quite different. That this is so could be seen from the consideration that the modified statement – 'I judge that S is P' – is not even an equivalent of the original 'S is P,' for the latter may be true while the former is false.

16.2.   Another way one could interpret the expressions under consideration as being equivalent to statements or at least as containing statements, is as follows. In so far as I ask a question or express a wish even in solitary speech, I apprehend the question or the wish in inner perception and then express the contents of those experiences in words. As a consequence, through my asking a question I am giving expression to my inner perception of the appropriate experience and thus I am also judging or making a statement; though not an ordinary predicative statement, the statement is the simple positing of that which is apprehended in inner perception.

A possible objection to this interpretation would run on already familiar tracks. It might be argued that the situation is not different in the case of statements. Could it not likewise be said that when I make a statement, I am putting into words not only

[1] *L.U.*, II, 2, p. 212.

the representations underlying the judgment but my 'inner perception' of the judgment itself, so that the meaning of the statement lies in the simple positing judgment about this inner perception of the first judgment? This however is not – according to this objection – the right interpretation of any sentence, not to speak of those making statements. Expressions are not names of experiences, unless of course the experience concerned is itself made the object of reflective awareness. When I say 'Gold is yellow,' I am not naming my representations corresponding to the terms 'gold,' 'is,' 'yellow,' but am in fact describing a state of affairs (*Sachverhalt*); I am *saying about* the metal gold. When actually wishing, I do not use words to *name* my wish. On the other hand, the expression of my wish belongs to the concrete constitution of my living act of wishing. To judge *expressively* is to judge, and not to name. To wish *expressively* is to wish, and, likewise, not to name. Naming a judgment or a wish is not judging or wishing.

To this objection it might be replied by saying that although to name a wish is not *therefore* to wish, it is yet possible that when I wish *expressively* I am actually wishing *and also* naming my wish. Is it not true that to entertain a wish and *together with it* to name the wish is *also* to wish (and not merely to name)?

16.3.   The trend of the discussion in the above two sub-sections points in the direction of Husserl's own solution. If by judgment is meant predicative judgment, Husserl would agree with Aristotle in holding that the sentences under discussion are *not in all cases* expressions of judgments. But as we have already pointed out, Aristotle nevertheless obliterates the radical distinction between judging on the one hand and the non-objectifying intentional experiences on the other by allowing the latter to function in the same way as the objectifying experiences do, i.e. as 'carriers' of meaning. The radical difference between the two groups of intentional experiences however necessitates that the modes of their functioning as meaning-intending acts should be totally different. This latter difference is brought out by Husserl in the following manner:

(i) Whereas the acts *expressed* in names and statements function as meaning-intending (as well as meaning-fulfilling) *without* themselves being made objective (*gegenständlich*),

(ii) the acts *expressed* in wish-sentences, in questions or in imperatives, function as meaning-intending *only in so far as* they *are* made objective, i.e. in so far as they are apprehended in 'inner perception.' The latter, i.e., the 'inner perception' being an objectifying act is the real carrier of meaning.

It follows that if an act is said to be 'expressed' when that act is the 'bearer' of the meaning of the expression, then it is *not* the living desires, questions, orders etc., but their inner perceptions that are strictly speaking *expressed* through the grammatical forms under consideration.

16.4.   Husserl's determination to find in a question or a wish or an imperative *theoretical meaning* at all costs–even by appealing to the dubious notion of an objectifying 'inner perception' – is but another aspect of the same trend in his thought which we noticed in the preceding section in connection with the 'egocentric particulars,' and it might even be said, suffers from the same defects as well. Even if the question 'Is S P?' is reducible to 'I ask if S is P,' the egocentricity of the latter refuses to be idealised by being detached from the context.

C. DEPENDENT AND INDEPENDENT, COMPLETE AND INCOMPLETE MEANINGS

§ 17.   Quine has spoken of "a continuum of possible ontologies," "ranging from a radical realism at the one extreme, where even a left hand parenthesis or the dot of an "i" has some weird abstract entity as its designatum, to a complete nihilism at the other extreme." [1] The nihilist is one who repudiates everything, the concrete as well as the abstract, by construing all words indiscriminately as syncategorematic.[2] We are not interested at the moment in the ontological aspect of the problem. The problem for us is, whether all or only some or, perhaps no expressions have complete meanings.[3] A good example of what Quine has called "complete nihilism" in the passage quoted

---

[1] W. V. O. Quine, "Designation and Existence," *Journal of Philosophy*, 1939, Vol. xxxvi, p. 704–5.
[2] *ibid.*, p. 704.
[3] The phenomenological approach to this problem was contrasted with the ontological in § 14.

above is found in Ryle's writings. Referring to Russell's doctrine of incomplete symbols as "a half-hearted attempt to re-allocate certain expressions from the categorematic to the syncategorematic family," Ryle writes: "It was half-fledged because it still assumed that there were or ought to be some syntactically complete categorematic expressions, some 'logically proper names' ..." [1] Ryle is thereby emphasizing that there are *no* categorematic expressions, and that all expressions are syncategorematic. Where does Husserl stand in this continuum whose one extreme is represented by the view that all expressions are categorematic (I must confess, I do not know who ever held this view) and whose other extreme is represented by the view that all expressions are syncategorematic? Husserl is here a traditionalist inasmuch as he recognizes the distinction between the categorematic and the syncategorematic expressions as fundamental and refuses to obliterate the distinction in either of the two extreme ways. But in our times when new ideas are being fashionable it is often forgotten that the tradition did often stand on solid grounds.

17.1. Husserl starts by rejecting two opinions which were held by Bolzano and Marty respectively. Bolzano is supposed to have held the view that *every* expression, categorematic or syncategorematic, has its *own* meaning. If Bolzano had held simply this view, there is no reason, as we shall see, why Husserl should oppose his own position to Bolzano's. To Bolzano however is attributed the further view that every expression has its own *independent* meaning. Marty, on the other hand, held the view that some expressions, i.e. the syncategorematic ones, have no meanings at all of their own – not even what Husserl would call dependent meaning – and are merely *mitbedeutend*.

Husserl's own view, as contrasted with those of Bolzano and Marty is that although every expression has its own meaning, not every expression has independent meaning. The syncategorematic expressions have their own meanings no doubt, but their meanings are 'dependent' whereas those of categorematic expressions are 'independent.' What appears initially to be a

---

[1] G. Ryle, "Meaning and Necessity," *Philosophy*, 1949, p. 71.

merely grammatical distinction is now traced to a more fundamental distinction amongst meanings.[1]

There are two components of this position: the first is the view
that a syncategorematic expression, even taken by itself, has
its own meaning. The other component is the theory that the
meaning of a syncategorematic expression is a 'dependent' one.

(i) The position that a syncategorematic expression, even
taken by itself, has its own meaning is established:

(a) firstly, by an appeal to the evidence that an isolated syncategorematic expression is understood in a sense in which
other incomplete expressions, mere prefixes or suffixes like
'ing' or 'ed' or mere detached constituents of words like 'ea'·or
'fi' are not. 'If' or 'but' *are* expressions, wheras 'ing,' 'ed' and
'fi' are not. No doubt, these latter signs need completion, but the
manner in which such signs would have to enter into a whole in
order to constitute an expression is not in any way determinable.
The syncategorematic expressions no doubt resemble these signs
in so far as they also demand completion. But there are two
major points of difference which cannot be overlooked:

In the first place, a syncategorematic expression demands
completion only on the *basis* of a certain definite meaning
which it, even when isolated, conveys. The second point is a
consequence of this: the supplementation that is demanded is
partly determined by the intended meaning of the syncategorematic expression concerned.[2] The supplementation demanded
is no doubt indeterminate with regard to the content to be
introduced; but with regard to the form, it is thoroughly determined in the sense that all possible supplementations are
circumscribed by a priori laws.

(b) Another evidence in favour of the contention that a syncategorematic expression has its own meaning is provided by
reflection on the fact that a syncategorematic expression fulfils
the same meaning-function everywhere, that is to say, in all
different complexes in which it functions as a constituent.

It has however to be admitted that the meaning of an isolated
syncategorematic expression suffers from two essential limi-

---

[1] This is a good illustration of Husserl's general conception of the relation of
grammar with logic.
[2] *L.U.*, II, 1, p. 306.

tations: on the one hand, it is – in a sense which is soon to be specified – 'dependent' and claims supplementation. On the other hand, our understanding of it can never amount to an 'intuitive understanding.' To consider the second point for the present: though Husserl allows that an isolated syncategorematic expression possesses a meaning-intention, he nevertheless recognizes that this detached meaning-intention is not capable of 'fulfilment' except in relationship to a complex whole of meanings. If we wish to 'clarify,' i.e. to bring to fulfilment, the meaning-intention of the syncategorematic expression, we have to think of concrete wholes in which it functions as a constituent. If, for example, we wish to 'clarify' in the above sense the meaning of 'and' or of 'equal to,' there is no other way of doing that except by bringing to mind propositions or phrases of the form 'a = b' or 'a and b.' It should not be thought however – Husserl warns us – that the meaning of a syncategorematic expression is, for the above reason, 'dependent' only with regard to the 'fulfilled meaning,' and that it should be regarded as 'independent' in so far as its intended meaning is concerned. This would be false, for not only is an isolated syncategorematic expression incapable of meaning-fulfilment but its meaning-intention as well needs supplementation. Thus its meaning is incomplete from both sides.

(ii) Saying that the syncategorematic expressions (and their meanings) are dependent whereas the categorematic ones (and their meanings) are independent is liable to be confused with certain other distinctions. For there are various senses in which expressions could be 'incomplete' and therefore could be in need of supplementation. It is necessary that these different senses should be clearly distinguished.

To start with, we could set aside abbreviations like 'i.e.' or 'UNO' that need expansion, and broken expressions which need filling up of the gaps. Expressions, incomplete in any of these senses, raise no philosophical problem. The latter, i.e. broken expressions with empty gaps are not strictly speaking expressions at all.

Coming to a more genuine sense in which expressions could be incomplete, we distinguish between simple and compound expressions (as well as between simple and compound meanings).

It is easy to see that the two pairs of distinction: 'dependent-independent' and 'simple-compound' overlap each other. Compound expressions could express an unitary meaning and be dependent, while simple expressions could be independent. Likewise, simple expressions like 'and' are dependent and obviously there are compound independent expressions.

The dependence of expressions (or of meanings) is defined thus: A content is to be called 'dependent' if it cannot subsist except as a constituent of a bigger whole. Such inability has its a priori ground in, i.e., follows necessarily from the type of the content under consideration: from which it follows that to every case of 'dependence' as here defined there corresponds a necessary law of the form that a content of the type a could only subsist as a constituent of a whole of the type G $(a,\beta\ldots\mu)$, where $\beta\ldots\mu$ stand for determinate types of contents.[1] This general definition of 'dependent contents' is applicable to 'dependent meanings' as well. The words "cannot subsist except as a constituent of a bigger whole" should not however be construed to mean that a detached syncategorematic expression could not have its meaning; they merely suggest that the meaning of such an isolated expression *demands* its inclusion in a bigger whole of a certain type.

17.2.   The distinctions between dependent and independent meanings, simple and compound meanings, and between incomplete and complete meanings suggest a question of philosophical importance which can not here be bypassed. Do these distinctions with regard to expressions (and their meanings) exactly correspond to similar distinctions amongst the objects [2] meant or referred to? This question, quite apart from its intrinsic importance, also provides us with a vantage-ground for comparing Husserl's thought with the logical atomism that followed him.

Logical atomism believed – to put the matter crudely – that logical analysis of language should yield us a metaphysical insight into the nature of facts. More specifically, it believed that both language and facts could be analysed down to the

[1] *L.U.*, II, 1, p. 311.
[2] Using 'object' in a sense which includes the 'facts' of the Cambridge Philosophers.

simple, not further analysable elements. It further believed that there is a strict relation of correspondence between the simple expressions and the simple, atomic facts: "some real and non-conventional one-one picturing relation between the composition of the expression and that of the fact." [1]

Husserl would readily agree that there *are* simple meanings and that there are compound meanings consisting of the simple ones.[2] But he would not concede that simple meanings correspond to simple objects, or that complex meanings correspond to complex objects. Meaning is not a mere reflex of the object: the analogy of 'picturing' deceives.[3] This could be seen by the following considerations:

(*a*) Compound meanings could represent a simple object. For example, the expression 'simple object' (and its meaning as well) is compound, while its object is simple.

(*b*) Simple meanings could represent compound objects. Leaving aside examples whose simplicity or complexity is difficult to decide, the simple expressions 'something' and 'one' (and their meanings as well) refer to diverse objects including those that are complex.

(*c*) Where a compound meaning represents a compound object, there is not always a one-to-one relationship amongst the elements of the one and the elements of the other. Husserl cites Bolzano's example of 'The country without a hill' in support of this contention.

Not only is there no strict correspondence between meanings and objects, there is also the lack of a similar correspondence between expressions and their meanings. For although each expression has its own meaning, the simplicity or complexity of expressions does *not* always 'picture' the simplicity or complexity of meanings. Husserl therefore goes on to ask the further question: how to decide whether the meaning of a given ex-

---

[1] G. Ryle, "Systematically Misleading Expression," *Proceedings of the Aristotelian Society*, 1931–32.

[2] "*Finden wir nun in einer Teil-Bedeutung abermals Teil-Bedeutungen, so mögen auch in diesen wieder Bedeutungen als Teile auftreten; aber offenbar kann dies nicht in infinitum fortgehen. Schliesslich werden wir in fortgesetzter Teilung überall auf einfache Bedeutungen als Elemente stossen müssen*" (*L.U.*, II, 1, 296).

[3] "*... dies Gleichnis vom Abbilde hier wie in manchen anderen Fällen trügt, und dass der vorausgesetzte Parallelismus nach keiner Seite besteht*" (*L.U.*, II. 1, 296). Further, "*die Idee eines gewissermassen bildartigen Ausdrückens ganz unbrauchbar ist*" (*L.U.*, II, 2, p. 134).

pression is simple or compound?[1] This question needs special treatment in connection with proper names and shall be discussed in the next section. It should, however, be mentioned here that an unqualified answer to the question whether the meaning of a given expression is simple or compound is rendered impossible by equivocation of the words 'simple' and 'complex' when applied to meanings. This equivocation may be brought out in the following manner:[2]

Simplicity or complexity may be attributed to the meaning itself, i.e. to the intended meaning as such. Or, it may be attributed to our consciousness of meaning, to the representations through which the identical meaning presents itself. Now, the case of proper names shows that simplicity in one sense does not exclude complexity in another. The meaning of the name of a person I know certainly is simple in the sense of retaining an identity in the midst of my changing 'representations' of him, for I mean that person and none other. But as I think of him more, new aspects and traits of his character appear in my mind and thus I have what might be called an articulate (gegliedert) consciousness of the meaning of his name. The meaning of a proper name though simple in one sense, is complex in another. It is simple in the sense that it means *the* person as it were in 'one ray'; in another sense, the meaning-consciousness develops through a 'many-rayed' intention of the form "the E who is a, the Ea who is b, the Eab who is c, ..."

With regard to other substantive and adjective words like 'man,' 'virtue', 'right' etc., Husserl rightly recognizes [3] that the simplicity or complexity of their meanings cannot be deduced from their logical definitions, for the logical definition is nothing but a merely practical artifice which hardly succeeds in really limiting the meaning or in organizing it from within.

Similar remarks may be made with regard to the dependence or independence of meanings. It has been said that the categorematic expressions refer to independent meanings whereas syncategorematic expressions refer to dependent meanings. But here again no correlation can be established between expressions

[1] *L.U.*, II, 1, p. 297–8.
[2] *L.U.*, II, 1, p. 298–300.
[3] *ibid.*, p. 301.

and their objects. The categorematic expression, 'dependent content,' itself is a good example of the point under consideration, for the expression though categorematic refers to a dependent object. It is possible to make dependent objects the objects of independent expressions by an indirect process. The colour red is a dependent object but may be referred to by the independent expression 'redness.'

Whatever might be the value of Husserl's own positive analysis, it cannot to-day be denied that his was a correct insight when he wrote, "the meaning certainly "represents" an objective, but it has not for the reason the character of a picture. Its essence lies rather in a certain intention, which can be intentionally "directed" upon any and everything, independent and dependent. And likewise can any and everything be made objective by way of meaning, i.e. can be made into an intentional object." [1] We must also recognize, firstly, that Husserl did not succumb to that illusion from which the logical atomists suffered; and secondly, that his own general attitude towards the relationship between grammar and logic should be subjected to the qualifications implied in the above discussions. For he is saying not merely that meanings do not picture objects, but also that expressions do not always tell us whether their meanings are simple or compound, dependent or independent.

D. THE CONCEPT OF NAME

§ 18. Names in the widest sense are said to be "expressions for representations" (*Ausdrücke von Vorstellungen*).[2] Further, nouns as such are not the same as names.[3] Names again are of two kinds: those that posit the named objects as existing, and those that do not so posit.[4] Finally, the distinction between names and statements is shown to be fundamental and undeniable.[5] Each of these points needs explication.

---

[1] *L.U.*, II, 1, p. 314: "*die Bedeutung zwar ein Gegenständliches "vorstellt," aber darum noch nicht den Charakter eines Abbildes hat; sondern dass ihr Wesen vielmehr in einer gewissen Intention liegt, die eben in der Weise der Intention auf alles und jedes, auf Selbständiges und Unselbständiges "gerichtet" sein kann.*"

[2] *ibid.*, pp. 462 f.

[3] *ibid.*, p. 463.

[4] *ibid.*, p. 464.

[5] *ibid.*, pp. 466–471.

(i) Names are *Ausdrücke von Vorstellungen*. The word '*Vor-stellung*' or 'representation' is ambiguous. It may mean – using Husserl's highly technical terminology [1] – either a complete intentional experience with its own distinctive 'act-quality' (and 'act-matter'), or the mere completed 'act-matter,' or finally any act (i.e. intentional experience) in which something or other is – in a certain narrow sense – objectified for us. These three senses of the word '*Vorstellung*' should be clearly distinguished before a proper appreciation of Husserl's account of names is possible. It should be borne in mind that names are expressions of *Vorstellungen* only in the last mentioned sense.

Husserl is trying to expound and interpret Brentano's principle: "Every intentional experience is either itself a *Vorstellung* or is founded upon *Vorstellungen*." [2] The principle owes its obviousness to the fact that an object in order to be judged, desired etc., i.e. in order to be made the object of an intentional experience, must be, at first, represented. In other words, unless an object is made the object of representation, it cannot be made the object of judgment or of desire, or of a feeling: from which it follows that intentional experiences like judging, desiring, feeling, wishing, are not independent, but are 'founded' (or dependent) experiences. *Vorstellung* or representation, on the other hand, is an independent intentional experience, not founded upon any prior experience. Examples of mere representations, taken as complete experiences, are: cases of merely imaginative representations in which the represented object is represented neither as existent nor as non-existent and cases of mere understanding in which the proposition understood is neither believed in nor disbelieved.

So far the interpretation of Brentano's principle presents no major difficulty. Husserl however goes on to draw a distinction between two senses of the word 'representation.' By 'representation' may be meant a complete intentional experience, complete with its distinctive act-quality and act-matter; it is complete in the same sense in which a judgment, a wish or a question is so. This is the sort of experience one has when one 'merely' under-

---

[1] A complete intentional experience, in accordance with Husserl's analysis, consists of a matter and a certain quality.

[2] *Op. cit.*, p. 427 f. Compare Russell's Principle of Reducibility to Acquaintance.

stands a word or when one 'merely' understands a statement or a question without himself judging or asking the question.

In the other sense, 'representation' means not an intentional experience, i.e. not a completed act but only the act-matter which is the foundation of all intentional acts, not excluding the *act* of representation itself. It is representation in this second sense that enters into other higher acts as their material basis.

Brentano's principle should be understood in the light of this distinction. The issue might be formulated thus: does the *matter* of an act of judgment, or that which makes a judgment to be a judgment *about this Sachverhalt*, lie in an act of representation?

There is no doubt that corresponding to every judgment there is a representation having the same matter as the judgment. Corresponding to a judgment 'S is P,' there is a 'mere' representation ('mere' understanding) of the sentence. But saying this does not amount to saying that the act of representation itself is a constituent of the act of judging. It is, of course, again true that the mere representation might be succeeded by a judgment or even that the judgment builds itself upon the representation. But by no means it follows that the original act of representation itself is included within the judgment as one of its constituents. It is to be conceded that as the act of judgment grows out of, or builds itself upon the representation, something is identically retained, something that was the matter of the original act of representation is taken over into the new act. But this identical something is far from being the original act itself. With the appearance of the new act, the original act is in fact dissolved, what is taken over as a constituent of the new act is only the *matter* of the original act. Judgment does *not* consist in the act of belief *plus* the mere understanding or representation of the proposition. The mere understanding has given place to a totally new act, directed towards the same matter though.

Brentano's principle may now be shown to be based upon an equivocation. When it is said that every intentional experience is either itself a representation or is founded upon representations, the first part of the principle speaks of representation in the sense of a completed act while the second part speaks of representation in the sense of act-matter alone. When an intentional experience is said to be itself a representation, the word 'representation' is used in the first sense. When on the other hand it is said that intentional experiences are based on representations, or have representations for their foundation, by 'representations' are meant only the act-matters. Thus the obviousness of the principle is found to be deceptive. Husserl is not satisfied with the principle as thus stated, but goes further ahead to give it a more tenable formulation. This new, and more tenable formulation is based upon a new concept of representation.

In this new and indeed the widest possible sense of the term, 'representation' means any *objectifying* intentional experience, that is to say any act in which something is made objective for us "in a certain narrower sense." What Husserl has in his mind is the manner in which something is 'grasped' all at once, or in which something objective is *meant* in one 'ray of meaning.'

Take the predicative judgment 'S is P' in which something is represented as being or not being something. But a quite different representation of the same is expressed by the expression – 'the being P of S.' The same situation again is made objective in a still different manner when we say 'That S is P is doubtful.'

Using 'representation' *in this widest sense*, Husserl formulates Brentano's principle thus: every intentional experience is either itself a representation or is founded upon one or more representations. Examples for the first part are the 'one-rayed' acts of perception, memory, expectation, imagination. Examples for the second part are the predicative judgments and even the corresponding cases of 'mere representations' in the sense explained above. A judgment has for its foundation at least one representation! The same may be expressed also by saying that a full statement must contain at least one name. Names are expressions of representations in this widest sense.

The following table of classification of intentional experiences should help us in understanding Husserl's analysis:

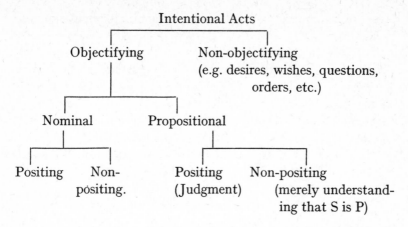

Intentional Acts

Objectifying — Non-objectifying (e.g. desires, wishes, questions, orders, etc.)

Nominal — Propositional

Positing — Non-positing. | Positing (Judgment) — Non-positing (merely understanding that S is P)

Husserl wants to establish two points: first, all non-objectifying acts are based on objectifying acts, for the objectifying acts are said to be the "primary bearer of matter" (*primärer Träger der Materie*).[1] All matter, be it of a question or of a wish or of an order, must be given through an objectifying act. Further, among objectifying acts, the propositional acts (i.e. predicative thoughts) are in the long run based on the nominal acts (i.e. presentations in the third of the above-mentioned senses of the term '*Vorstellung*'). This gives to names their undeniably fundamental importance.

18.1. (ii) Recent discussions of the problem are marked by a striking suspicion of the entire category of names. Reference has been made to this in § 17. Quine, amongst others, has suggested that names should be construed as descriptions. "Instead of treating the ostensively learned word as a *name of* the shown object to begin with," writes Quine, "we treat it to begin with as a predicate *true* exclusively of the same object; then we construe the name, as such, as amounting to "(ix) Fx" where "F" represents that primitive predicate..."[2] What Quine proposes is nothing but a more thorough application of Russell's principle of reducing ordinary proper names to definite descriptions. Russell's 'logically proper names' are not immune

[1] *L.U.*, II, I, pp. 493-4.
[2] W. V. O. Quine, *Methods of Logic*, New York, 1951, p. 218-9.

from this reductionism. They too can be eliminated by paraphrase 'à la Russell.' "Whatever we say with the help of names can be said in a language which shuns names altogether." [1]

Connected with this Russell-Quine movement, but quite distinct from it, is the Frege-Wittgenstein-Rylean insistence on the fact that names are abstractions from sentences. Names do not logically precede sentences; they are not categorematic, in fact no expression is so. Their original home is in sentences.

It is indeed interesting to be reminded, in such hostile circumstances, of Husserl's insistence on the irreducibility and basic importance of names.

To begin with, it must be mentioned even at the cost of repetition that Husserl is not confusing meaning with naming. If he did, he would not have distinguished between names and other expressions. He would have in fact treated all meaningful expressions as names. Far from doing so, he even sees that a mere noun as such does not name. [2] A name must be a complete symbol, or in Husserl's language, must give expression to a self-contained intentional experience. If an expression be a name, in other words, if it expresses a self-contained intentional experience, it must in that case be able to fulfil the subject-function of a statement without any change in its nature. To be able to satisfy this requirement, a noun must be coupled at least with a definite or an indefinite article. 'Man' is not a name, 'The man in a grey suit' is one. [3]

There are several possible ways of obliterating this distinction between names and statements. It might be said that names 'arise' out of judgments and therefore refer back to them. Or, it might be argued that a whole statement might function as a name.

To the argument that a large number of names 'arises' out of prior judgments and therefore refer back to them, Husserl replies [4] by pointing out that an appeal to such an 'origin' does not really serve to abolish the distinction. The name 'S that is

---

[1] W. V. O. Quine, *From a Logical Point of View*, Harvard, 1953, p. 13.

[2] *L.U.*, II, 1, pp 462–3.

[3] An adjective also is not a name, though an adjective can be 'nominalized.' In the latter cases it has to undergo modification. The original function of an adjective is predicative and attributive. But when nominalized as in 'Green is a colour,' it functions as a name (*L.U.*, II, 1, p. 324–5).

[4] *L.U.*, II, 1, pp. 468–470.

P' might have grown out of the predicative judgment 'S is P'; but to say this is not to say that the name is reducible to the statement. For the nominal representation has its own peculiar character which is totally different from anything belonging to predicative thought. The nominal representation might be a modification of the original predicative thought; but the original is not 'contained in' the modified form. The modified form is something totally new.

A whole statement might, no doubt, function as a name, for example in sentences like 'That the price of rice is now cheap is bound to please most men' (generally speaking, in sentences of the form "That S is P is . . ."). In order to be able to appreciate the nature of such cases, we must distinguish between (a) stating a fact, (b) naming a fact, and (c) naming a judgment.[1] That it is easy to confuse these three hardly needs to be pointed out.

The statement 'S is P' does not name, but only states the fact that S is P.[2] But when we say 'That S is P is gratifying,' we are not merely stating the fact (that S is P), we are in fact naming it. It should be seen that in sentences like 'That S is P is gratifying,' we are naming, not the original judgment, but the fact originally stated; what is gratifying is not the judgment that S is P, but the fact that S is P. But it is also possible to name the judgment, as for example, when we say 'The judgment 'S is P' is categorical, affirmative, etc. etc.

These distinctions teach us that when a whole statement functions as a name, it ceases to state. It names. There is no reason therefore for suspecting that the distinction between naming and stating is thereby abolished.

This very important difference between naming a fact and stating a fact is further explained by Husserl in the following manner. The same fact is objectified in two different ways. In the one case when the fact is *named*, the entire fact with all its inner complexity is grasped all at once, in one ray of consciousness as it were. When the same fact is *stated or judged*, there is a many-rayed awareness, a synthetic awareness in which many

---

[1] *L.U.*, II, 1, p. 460; pp. 471-2.
[2] Compare G. Ryle: ". . . Sentences are not names. Saying is not naming." ("The Theory of Meaning" in Mace, *loc. cit.*, p. 254).

constituent representations are brought into an unity. The mode
of consciousness is in each case different. The one-rayed apprehension of the fact that S is P no doubt presupposes the many-
rayed awareness which makes possible the statement 'S is P';
nevertheless the name is phenomenologically different from the
statement out of which it 'arises.' Naming and stating are therefore not merely grammatically different, but essentially different
(*wesensverschieden*).[1]

18.2. (iii) The *Wesensverschiedenheit* between naming and
stating cannot however be fully appreciated so long as the
concept of name is not further widened. A statement is a 'positing' propositional act; to state is to 'posit.' (Understanding
a statement is not positing, though.) Names may be positing or
they may be non-positing. The admission of non-positing names
of course runs counter to the more recent ideas on this issue,
and here again it might be possible to show that his case is not
as bad as it would *prima facie* appear to be.

Russell has argued that the designatum of a name *must* be
something with which we are acquainted. Existence cannot be
denied of what is named without involving self-contradiction.
Where therefore there is denial of existence as, e.g., in 'The
present king of France does not exist,' the subject term is not
a name but a description. In Husserl's language, all names are
bound to be positing. The notion of a non-positing name should
be on this view self-contradictory.

Husserl agrees that a name names a *Vorstellung* – with the
obvious qualification that his use of '*Vorstellung*' is wider than
Russell's use of 'Acquaintance.' But Russell, it might be urged,
fails to keep apart the phenomenological and the ontological
issues. To say that a name names a representation and to say that
the named, i.e., the represented must exist are two different things.
It is still another thing to claim that a name must name the represented object *as existent*. Where the name is positing, that is to
say, the nominal representation represents the object named
qua existent, Russell's theory is valid, further affirmation of
existence is superfluous, and denial of it self-contradictory. But
where the nominal representation is as such non-positing, the

[1] *L.U.*, II, 1, p. 477.

predication of existence may subsequently come forward as a synthetic act. Perception, memory, expectation, and judgments – strictly speaking, the corresponding nominal representations – are positing. Illusory representations when they are free from any stand regarding the reality of what appears, merely phantasy-representations etc. are non-positing. Similarly, a *positing* propositional act, i.e. a judgment made by the speaker may be 'merely understood' – without being believed in or disbelieved – by the hearer and then modified into a nominal representation which would in consequence be *non-positing*. It is obvious that Husserl's recognition of the possibility of non-positing names is due to the wide sense in which he uses the term 'nominal representation.'

18.3.   (iv) A nominal representation, further, need not be simple or atomic, though it should be, as said before, one-rayed. A complex synthetic judgment may be modified into a nominal representation by being grasped all at once in one one-rayed act of awareness. Thus Husserl is free from that atomistic conception of names which vitiated logical atomism. Names do not owe their distinctive character to anything in the object named; they owe it *rather to the peculiar mode of consciousness* in which the object is represented. Here is another example of how Husserl keeps phenomenology and ontology apart.

As a consequence, Husserl is not prepared to grant that even proper names (he need not, quite understandably, distinguish between ordinary proper names and logically proper names) should have a simple meaning. All talk about simplicity and complexity here as elsewhere is full of equivocations: simplicity in one sense does not exclude complexity in another. The meaning of a proper name, say, of a person, is certainly simple in the sense that the name refers to an identical person in the midst of changing representations. On the other hand, the changing representations are also essential, for it is through them that our consciousness of the meaning of the name develops.[1]

Husserl goes on to add that even the meaning of a proper name has a generality of its own.[2] This generality is of a totally

---

[1] *L.U.*, II, 1, pp. 297 ff.
[2] *L.U.*, II, 2, pp. 30–1.

different sort, though, from the generality of the meaning of class names. For does not a proper name retain an identity of meaning in the midst of varying representations? The same person may be perceived, imagined, remembered, expected etc. And in each case many different perspectives are there. But the name names the same person.

As in the case of all other names, so also here, *to name* an object as X and *to know* it as X are synonymous expressions.[3] To say 'the name 'red' names the red object red' and to say 'The red object is known as red, and through such knowledge is named 'red'' are saying the same thing. To name a person 'Ram' or a city 'Cuttack' is also to know the person *as* Ram or to know the city *as* Cuttack.

The generality of a proper name consists in the fact that corresponding to the object named there is a synthesis of possible perceptions which possess a common intentional character. This common intentional character is what relates each such perception to the same object, notwithstanding the *phenomenal* differences amongst the perceptions.

The generality of a class name, on the other hand, consists in an extension of objects, to each one of which there corresponds again a possible synthesis of perceptions in the manner described above.

[1] *L.U.*, II, 2, pp. 28; 30.

CHAPTER VI

FORMAL LOGIC

§ 19.   Our task in this chapter is (i) to undertake a delimitation of the frontier of formal logic within the total realm of thought and further, (ii) to study the exact nature of this discipline along with its inner stratifications and outer ramifications. In connection with formal logic Husserl was chiefly preoccupied with these two problems. What he has given us therefore in his *Logische Untersuchungen* and the *Formale und transzendentale Logik* is not a system of logic but a systematic *meta*-logic.

Logic is concerned with meanings.[1] This by itself however is too vague a statement to enlighten us. Several preliminary distinctions have to be borne in mind. To start with, Nonsense (*Unsinn*) is not the same as countersense (*Widersinn*).[2] The distinction between meaningfulness and meaninglessness is not the same as that between meaningfulness and the character of possessing contradictory meaning. Both distinctions, it is obvious, concern sequences of expressions, and therefore pertain to relations of compatibility or incompatibility among meanings. There are however two radically different sorts of compatibility or incompatibility among meanings. The idea of *Unsinn* refers to one kind of incompatibility, and the idea of *Widersinn* to another.

The one kind of incompatibility is illustrated in such meaningless sequences as 'round if,' 'man but and if.' The other kind of incompatibility is illustrated in sequences like 'round square,' 'S is not S' etc. It is only the latter kind of incompatibility which exhibits what is generally called 'logical' contradiction. Now, according to Husserl, the laws governing the former kind of incompatibility should also come under the scope of formal

---

[1] Even Carnap writes: "I no longer believe that a logic of meaning is superfluous." (*Introduction to Semantics*, p. 249).

[2] *L.U.*, II, 1, pp. 326 f.

logic. 'Pure logical grammar,' which according to Husserl dis-
cusses the laws determining the permissible combinations and
modifications of meaning, forms the lowest stratum of formal
logic.

The component meanings of 'round square' no doubt form one
unitary meaning, whereas the component meanings of 'round or'
refuse to unite by virtue of a purely grammatical incompatibility.
What however is lacking in the case of 'round square' is the
possibility of fulfilment of the complex meaning-intention. The
possibility of meaning-fulfilment is ruled out a priori. Logical
incompatibility in the narrow sense, i.e. in the sense of logical
contradiction, does not therefore prevent the formation of a
unitary meaning-intention: the self-contradictory expression
still carries sense. It is grammatical incompatibility which
renders all unitary significance impossible.

If we further ask why is it that certain sequences of words
in a language make sense while others do not, Husserl's answer
comes to depart radically from that of most contemporary
philosophers in the English-speaking world [1] (which however is
no reason why Husserl's answer should not deserve serious
attention.) Incidentally, we also come to touch upon the problem
of the relation of logic to grammar.

Most English-speaking philosophers of today, leaving aside the
devotees of ordinary language, would agree in condemning the
grammar of ordinary language as an unsafe guide in drawing
logical distinctions. The traditional parts of speech, they hold, are
but merely crude approximations to truly syntactical categories.
A truly logical syntax cannot therefore be based upon the
grammar of ordinary language, but, in order to be *pure* syntax,
must be a conventionally constructed set of rules of formation
and transformation. Bearing this contemporary attitude in mind
let us now turn to Husserl's answer to the question: why is it
that certain sequences of words in a language make sense while
others do not?

19.2. Husserl's answer is suggested in the following paragraph:

[1] Compare Y. Bar-Hillel, "Husserl's Conception of a Purely Logical Grammar,"
Philosophy and Phenomenological Research, 1956-7, pp. 362-9.

"If we enquire into the reasons why certain combinations are permitted and certain others prohibited in our language, we shall be, in a very great measure, referred to accidental linguistic habits and, in general, to facts of linguistic development that are different with different linguistic communities. But, in another part, we meet with the essential distinction between independent and dependent meanings, as also with the a priori laws – essentially connected with that distinction – of combination of meanings and of meaning modifications: laws that must more or less clearly exhibit themselves in the theory of grammatical forms and in a corresponding class of grammatical incompatibilities in every developed language." [1]

This passage bears testimony to Husserl's belief that although each language has its accidental features, its grammatical rules, its syntactical laws that it does not share with some other languages, yet underlying such accidental features there is a universal logical grammar whose distinctions and laws determine, to a large measure, the grammar and the syntax of every developed language. [2]

Husserl, it must be said, nowhere proves convincingly that there *is* such a universal logical grammar underlying the accidental and varying features of the different languages. It might however be possible to argue that since it is possible *to translate* one language into another, to say what is said in one language in another, there must therefore be *a common logical basis*. [3] And this common logical basis must be more elementary and more primitive than what is ordinarily known as 'formal logic.' Why not then call it the basis or the lowest stratum of 'formal logic'? Taken by itself, this common logical basis could be called, with equal justification, either a pure logical grammar or a pure logical syntax.

Thus, in his idea of the *relation between grammar and logic*, [4] Husserl sought to steer clear of two extreme views. [5] At one

---

[1] *L.U.*, II, 1, p. 327–8.

[2] Compare: "*Wieviel vom tatsächlichen Inhalt der historischen Sprachen, sowie von ihren grammatischen Formen in dieser Weise empirisch bestimmt sein mag, an dieses ideale Gerüst ist jede gebunden....*" (*ibid.*, p. 338–9).

[3] I am indebted to Professor Kalidas Bhattacharyya of the Viswa-Bharati University for this suggestion.

[4] Compare, *L.U.*, II, 1, pp. 2; 12–14; 294–5; 341–2.

[5] In *F.u.t.L.*, p. 62, he says that in the *Formenlehre*, "*die Leitung durch die Grammatik (was an historisch faktische Sprachen und ihre grammatische Deskription erinnern soll)*" is replaced by "*die Leitung durch das Grammatische selbst.*"

extreme, there is an almost naive faith in ordinary grammar
as a safe guide to logical distinctions; at the other extreme, there
is an equally naive distrust of grammar leading to artificially
constructed systems of syntax as the basis of logic. Husserl is
well aware that ordinary grammar may deceive. While it is
certainly important constantly to bear in mind the possibility
of such deception, we should at the same time also remember
that there are grammatical distinctions that are based upon
relevant distinctions amongst meanings and meaning-modifications.

19.3.   The task of a pure logical grammar [1] is to lay down
(i) the primitive forms of meanings, or, pure *categories* of
    meanings;
(ii) the primitive forms of *composition* of meanings;
(iii) the primitive forms of *modification* of meanings;
(iv) the pure *syntactical* categories;
(v) the laws of *operation* with meanings by virtue of which new,
    more complex meanings could be constructed; and finally
(vi) to construct "a closed system of basic forms" [2] of meanings,
    based upon "a minimum number of independent elementary
    laws," [3] which would make possible a systematic survey of
    the plurality of all possible forms of meaning, deducible by
    continued application of the laws of composition and modi-
    fication.[4]

(i) The primitive forms or *categories of meaning* are, for example, the nominal, the adjectival, and the propositional
meanings. Of these, it is only the propositional meaning which
is independent; all other forms of meanings are possible constituents of the full propositional meaning.[5] It is in this sense that
a theory of propositional forms includes the entire theory of
forms of meanings, for every concrete meaning is either itself a
proposition or a possible constituent of a proposition. Pure
logical grammar would thus not only simply classify propositions,
but demonstrate "the bare *possibility* of propositions as propo-

---

[1] *L.U.*, II, 1, pp. 328–330.
[2] *F.u.t.L.*, p. 44.
[3] *L.U.*, II, 1, p. 328.
[4] *L.U.*, II, 1, pp. 329–30.
[5] *ibid.*, pp. 329–30.

sitions, without concerning itself with the question, if they are true or false, consistent or self-contradictory." [1] It is obvious that this possibility is *not* the same as what is *ordinarily* called 'logical' possibility, for the ordinary notion of 'logical' possibility involves the notion of logical contradiction which belongs, as mentioned before, to an upper stratum of logic. We are concerned here with something more primitive.

(ii) To the primitive *forms of composition* (*Verknüpfungs-formen*) belong, for example,[2] the forms of conjunction, disjunction, the form 'If-then,' the attributive and the predicative forms. It might of course be objected at this point that Husserl was wrong in treating all these forms as if they were equally primitive, whereas some of them are definable in terms of others. Actually however there is nothing in such a possibility which could prevent us from recognizing the soundness of Husserl's general idea of a logical grammar. In fact, Husserl did recognize the possibility of reducing the number of primitive forms to a minimum, so that the others might be deducible from the primitive ones by "pure construction." [3]

Husserl does not fail to notice that we are not entirely free in forming meaningful compositions of meanings.[4] Taking a meaningful combination and by *formalising* it, we get what Husserl calls a '*Formidee*': 'p and q,' 'p or q,' 'If p, then q,' 'S is P' are such *Formideen*. Now, it is easy to see that although it is possible to *materialize* these forms in many different ways by replacing the variables by nonlogical words, yet we are not entirely free in this respect. Not any and every nonlogical word could be substituted either for S or for p or for q. It is only meanings belonging to a fixed category that could replace a variable in a '*Formidee*'; insert a meaning from a different category, e.g. an adjective in the subject-place of the form 'S is P,' and the result would be simple nonsense. "By free exchange of matter within the same category, there might result false, stupid, ridiculous meanings (either whole propositions or possible constituents of propositions), but necessarily unitary meanings, that is to say, grammatical expressions whose meaning permits

[1] *F.u.t.L.*, p. 44.
[2] *L.U.*, II, 1, p. 330.
[3] *ibid.*, p. 333.
[4] *ibid.*, pp. 317–320.

itself to be "executed" in an unitary manner. As soon as we transgress the categories, that is no more the case."[1] Husserl is thereby clearly anticipating Russell's theory of types.

(iii) It might be pointed out as against the above categorial restriction that meanings belonging to any category do in fact function in the subject place of the form 'S is P.' In 'Green is a colour,' an adjectival meaning is meaningfully functioning as the subject. Similarly, in "'and' is a conjunction," a syncategorematic expression fulfils the same function. Is not then the categorial restriction useless?

The objection however fails to take notice of the very important phenomenon of *meaning-modification*.[2] The adjectival meaning is not simply transplanted into a place to which only the nominal could legitimately belong. The adjectival undergoes a modification. The word remains the same, no doubt; but the meaning is not quite the same. Nor is the meaning entirely transformed, the original meaning completely abandoned. There is a *core* of meaning which is retained unchanged in spite of the modification of the adjectival into the nominal meaning. Husserl often says that the modification concerns the *syntactical* form.[3] Of his notion of syntax we shall have occasions to speak later on.

Similarly, an entire proposition can also be nominalised. In 'That S is P is an agreeable proposition,' the nominalised propositional meaning functions as the subject.

It is Husserl's contention that even such meaning-modifications are subject to a priori laws, laws that are rooted in the nature of the various regions of meaning and in accordance with which meanings undergo modifications to give rise to new meaning-forms while retaining an identical core.[4]

One could also show how a propositional form, say, the form 'S is P' is capable of a series of modifications: 'S which is P...' 'If S is P, ...,' 'So is S P,' 'S may be P,' 'S must be P' etc. etc. In such cases we have an *Urform* or a primitive form, and a whole multiplicity of modifications, derivable from it by construction.[5]

[1] *ibid.*, p. 319.
[2] *L.U.*, II, 1, *Unt.* IV, § 11; *F.u.t.L.*, § 13b.
[3] *L.U.*, II, 1, p. 325.
[4] *ibid.*, p. 324.
[5] *F.u.t.L.*, § 13 (b).

(iv) Some of these modifications are modal, and some syntactical.[1] When, for example, the predicative proposition 'S is P' is modified into 'Is S P?' or, 'S may be P' etc., the modification is modal. When, however, the entire proposition is nominalised in the form 'That S is P is...,' or when an adjective is nominalised as in 'Green is a colour' or when an adjective takes up the attributive in place of the predicative function as in 'The green grass...,' the modification is said to be syntactical. (Such syntactical modifications are said to give rise to new kinds of objectivities called syntactical objectivities. The nominalisation of the proposition 'S is P' gives rise to the *fact* that S is P. Nominalisation of the adjective 'green' gives rise to the new kind of syntactical objectivity called 'property.'[2] The study of such objectivities, as of other similar objectivities, belongs not to formal logic but to formal ontology.)[3]

19.4. It must be admitted that Husserl's use of the term 'syntax' is not quite fixed. Further, his use of it is different from the linguist's.[4] We could say that he is concerned with *logical syntax*. Logical syntax in the strict sense should be coextensive with the entire pure logical grammar, instead of being, as Husserl often gives us to understand, a part of it. Strictly speaking, therefore, the study of the pure categories of meaning, of the permissible forms of connection as well as modification, should all belong to logical syntax. Nor is 'logical syntax' in Husserl's sense the same as Carnap's 'logical syntax': Carnap's is a purely formalised theory in the sense of being built up on conventions. Further, Carnap's theory avoids all reference to designata and includes besides the theory of formal deduction.[5] Husserl's

---

[1] cp. *Ideen*, p. 327.

[2] "*Unter syntaktischen Gegenständlichkeiten verstehen wir solche, die aus anderen Gegenständlichkeiten durch "syntaktische Formen" abgeleitet sind.*" (*Ideen*, p. 29). "*Jeder in sich abgeschlossene prädikative Urteilssatz konstituiert also in sich eine neue Gegenständlichkeit vor, einen Sachverhalt.*" (*E.u.U.*, p. 288). "*Jeder Sachverhalt ist eine vollständige syntaktische Gegenständlichkeit.*" (*ibid.*, p. 290).

[3] See § 20.7 following.

[4] "*Dieser Begriff von Syntax und syntaktisch, der sich rein auf die logische Form bezieht, darf also nicht verwechselt werden mit den sprachwissenschaftlichen Begriffen von Syntax und syntaktischer Form.*" (*E.u.U.*, p. 247 fn.) The syntactical forms are elsewhere said to be 'synthetic,' involving synthetic *operations* of combining, modifying etc. (*Ideen*, p. 326).

[5] See Carnap's explanation of the word 'syntax' in Appendix to his *Introduction to Semantics*.

'logical syntax' is formal, *but not formalized* in the above sense; the reference to designata is avoided except in the sense that there are syntactical objectivities whose categories come under discussion in formal ontology. Lastly, logical syntax, according to Husserl, *does not include* the theory of formal deduction, since it constitutes only the lowest stratum of formal logic (the formal logic of deduction belonging to the next higher stratum of it). The reason for this last difference is, that whereas Carnap tends to identify formal logic with syntax, Husserl makes syntax the indispensable *foundation* of logic.[1]

Discussing Husserl's logical investigations to-day, it is instructive and interesting to watch the slow but significant change that has come about in Carnap's thoughts on logic. While in the *Logical Syntax of Language* (London & New York, 1937), logic is identified with syntax,[2] in the *Introduction to Semantics* (Cambridge, Mass, 1942), we are told that "logic... is a special part of Semantics." [3] "I now regard semantics," he writes, "as the fulfilment of the old search for a logic of meaning." [4] Husserl's notion of syntax cuts across the artificially created distinction between a formalized syntax and a formalized semantics, and thereby succeeds in a large measure in fixing the proper location of the logical.

19.5.   Husserl distinguishes between *syntactical form* and *syntactical stuff*.[5] Taking an expression and letting it function in different roles in sentences, e.g. as a subject and then as a predicate etc., we find that a core of meaning remains identical. Consider the two sentences 'This paper is white' and 'I am writing on this paper': the expression 'this paper' retains an identical *Sachbezüglichkeit*, a 'reference to the same,' in spite of the changing forms which it takes on. These two aspects could be separated only by abstraction, for every concrete expression has these two aspects in one. The ideas of 'pure form' and 'pure stuff' are therefore limiting concepts. We never have at first a

---

[1] For criticism of Carnap's identification of logic with syntax, see M. Black, *Problems of Analysis*, Cornell U.P., 1954, Ch. XIV.

[2] *Logical Syntax of Language*, pp. 233; 259.

[3] *Introduction to Semantics*, p. 56.

[4] *Introduction to Semantics*, p. 249.

[5] cp. especially *F.u.t.L.*, Beilage I. § 3.

pure stuff [1] to which we subsequently apply form. It is rather a previously formed meaning to which a new form is applied or whose syntactical form is modified, so that a given form becomes the stuff for new syntactical operations. Thus the distinction between form and matter – leaving aside the sense in which they are limiting notions – is relative. It also follows that it might be possible to distinguish between lower and higher forms. The higher forms are based upon the lower ones in the sense that they presuppose stuffs with lower forms. Thus, for example, the propositional form presupposes the subject-form and the predicate-form. A proposition has its own referentiality, the reference to a *Sachverhalt*; but the referentiality of a proposition is 'founded' in the sense that it is mediated by the referentiality of its constituent terms.

Further, while the number of syntactical stuffs that retain their identity is infinite, the number of syntactical forms is limited. While again it is true that every such stuff can admit of a wide range of formation, this range is in each case bound to be limited. That is to say, a given stuff can not admit of any and every syntactical form.

Again, there are some forms, e.g., the subject-form, that can appear at any stage of complication. An entire proposition can function as the subject of another proposition. But there are other forms, for example, the form 'If S is P, ...' or the form '..., then Q is R,' that, by their very nature, demand a complex structured stuff to be taken in.

Husserl next comes to distinguish between syntactical forms and non-syntactical forms, as also between corresponding stuffs.[2] The syntactical forms are forms of propositions or of constituents of propositions. Coming from propositions to their constituents and from these constituents to their constituents and proceeding in this manner one reaches the last stuff whose form is no more syntactical. Starting with the proposition, for example, 'The paper is white,' one comes to the subject-form 'the paper.' Abstracting again from the subject-form, (which is a syntactical form) one reaches the simple substantive 'paper'

---

[1] It must be borne in mind that Husserl is not speaking of 'pure stuff' in the Aristotelian sense of 'pure matter'. The distinction between stuff and form here is not ontological but logical, i.e., it concerns the sphere of meaning.

[2] *F.u.t.L.*, Beilage I, § 11.

which is, *syntactically considered*, a last unformed stuff. Though
free from syntactical form, it is however *not* entirely unformed
(for the conception of a pure stuff is, as said before, a merely
limiting conception). This is true not only of substantives like
'paper,' 'man,' but also of adjectives like 'white' 'round' etc.
What remain identical amidst variations in such cases, in other
words their forms, are not syntactical forms but non-syntactical
ones like the substantival or the adjectival forms. Thus whereas
the subject form, the predicate-form or the attributive form
are syntactical, the substantival and the adjectival forms are
non-syntactical.

It might be asked, why should we at all distinguish between
stuff and form at this pre-syntactical level? Husserl's reply is:
consider two pre-syntactical structures, 'red' and 'redness'; or
consider the pair 'similar' and 'similarity.' Now, in each of these
pairs, an identical stuff has taken two different non-syntactical
forms, in one case the adjectival and in the other the substantival.
If we abstract even from these forms, we reach the last stuff:
that, for example, which is common to both 'red' and 'redness,'
or to both 'similar' and 'similarity.' As we reach this level of
analysis and uncover the last 'element,' i.e. "*die Stoffe in dem
allerletzten Sinne*," we are possibly also leaving the realm of thought
and passing over into the realm of 'pre-predicative experience.'

At the lowest level then we have the last stuff (the so-called
'*Kernstoff*') which is subjected to the operations of the non-
syntactical forms (the so-called '*Kernform*'). From such operations
arise the structures (the so-called '*Kerngebilde*') which are the
materials for the syntactical operations. Syntactical operations
(as also syntactical forms), are again of various orders which
could roughly be classified into two. The syntactical forms of
the lower order are concerned with propositional *constituents*,
whereas those of the higher order are concerned with propositions.
Thus within the pure logical grammar, we have uncovered
further stratifications of phenomenological relevance.

Before developing further the idea of pure logical grammar we
shall pause to intersperse this account with another important
finding of Husserl. Amongst the non-syntactical forms, the
substantival form enjoys a specially privileged position.[1] This

---

[1] *F.u.t.L.*, Beilage I, § 13.

means that adjectives and relations can always be substantivised, whereas not every substantive can be adjectivised. When an adjective is substantivised – for example, when 'red' is transformed into 'redness' – the resulting substantive has a secondary, or in Husserl's language, a 'founded' meaning which refers back to the original adjectival meaning. This transformation of the non-syntactical structure, however, makes possible a syntactical transformation as for example of the proposition 'This leaf is green' into the proposition' Greenness is the colour of this leaf' etc. etc. In fact, as we have seen in connection with syntactical operations, every syntactical structure can be 'nominalised.'

Husserl has here made us *conscious* of an operational law which has been detested by many contemporary philosophers as a deliberate distortion. It has been pointed out by these philosophers that the metaphysician's love for substantivisation leads to the postulation of undesirable abstract entities. In fact, the entire category of substantive has come to be suspected as concealing a subtle metaphysical manoeuvre. It goes to Husserl's credit to have exhibited, as against this current opinion, firstly, that the possibility of substantivisation is grounded in the very nature of the categories concerned, i.e. that there is a certain necessity about this possibility which is lacking in the opposite possibility, say, of adjectivising all substantives; and secondly, that a substantivised adjective nevertheless refers back to the original adjectival meaning. This second point should dispel the fear of those who suspect that all substantivisation encourages the postulation of abstract entities.

He has also succeeded in throwing some new light on the concept of 'Term,' [1] which was left more or less vague and unclear in traditional logic. Take the following example of a syllogism from the older text-books of logic:

All men are mortal

All mortals are impermanent

All men are impermanent.

Here we have an identical middle term. The adjectival 'mortal' and the substantive 'mortals' are said to be the same 'term.' In view of the foregoing analysis, we could suggest that they are the same 'term' in the sense that they have the same primitive

---

[1] *F.u.t.L.*, pp. 273-4.

stuff, the same *Kernstoff*, though the non-syntactical categories are different in the two cases. One of the meanings of 'concept,' according to Husserl, is the socalled *Kernstoff*; in this sense, the 'term' may be said to be the 'concept.'

19.6.   The foregoing notion of syntax is capable of being extended from the theoretical (or *doxic*) to the practical and the affective spheres.[1] For example, the syntactic connective 'and' has its axiological and practical uses as well. Husserl's example is the following: a mother's loving glance at her children is a collective love that pertains to each child separately but also comprehends them all *in one act*. This one act is *not* analysable into an act of love plus a collective theoretical representation; the act of loving itself is collective. Objectively speaking, the beloved children form one collective object of love (and not merely one factual collection plus an added act of love directed towards them.)

Though in this way the syntactical operations have their parallels in the affective and the practical spheres, nevertheless the doxic syntax remains basic. It is in this sense – and only in this sense – that we have to understand Husserl's contention that the logical has a universality which does not belong to the affective or the practical.[2] Every act, we have already seen,[3] hides a predicative act, every statement a proposition. This indicates at once the source, and the limitation, of the universality of the logic of predicative propositions. Husserl, it hardly needs to be emphasized, is far from being a Hegelian pan-logist. All objectification, he would say, is due to a doxic act, i.e. a predicative judgment. So far as the affective and the practical sentences are objectifiable, they also involve predication and are so far subject to logical syntax. Otherwise, they constitute a domain apart.

19.7.   Two more notions belong to Husserl's idea of a pure logical grammar. One of these is the idea of operation and the other is the idea of a minimum number of primitive laws.[4] These two

---

[1] *Ideen*, p. 328. Also § 121 and pp. 359 ff.
[2] *Ideen* pp. 290–1; also p. 299.
[3] Compare § 16, Ch. V of this book.
[4] Compare § 19.3 above and the references given there.

notions if rightly understood would go a long way towards lessening the distance that separates Husserl's logical grammar from the modern notion of a system of syntax.[1]

Husserl speaks of the "point of view of 'operation'." It is possible, that is to say, to regard the system of pure logical grammar *as a construction* with the help of operational laws (rather than as a static, pre-given system of eternally accomplished connections). In that case, to each one of the various forms of composition and modification, there should correspond a certain operational law and an operational possibility. Further, these operational laws could be arranged in order of their logical priority, simplicity etc. Some operational forms can be regarded as the basic ones, others as developments or constructions out of them. The form 'S is P' is thus more primitive than the form 'S which is P is . . .' (It is even possible to regard 'S is P' itself as an operation.) To every operation again there may be assigned a corresponding law stating the possibility of its continued application (iteration), as for example, of the continued application of conjunction to generate such forms as 'S is P and Q and . . . .".

By recognizing that the system can be viewed as a construction and further by emphasizing the necessity of starting from a minimum number of primitive laws – howsoever one might choose them – Husserl counterbalances the impression of dogmatism that his idea of the system is likely to give at the first instance. At the same time it is true that he never fell into the opposite error of conventionalism.

It should further be noted that Husserl avoids all ontologising in this context, except for the fact that he would call any form of composition or modification that is sanctioned by the pure syntactical laws an *existent* one. That is to say, there is an *existential* theorem corresponding to each valid law of operation, composition or modification of meaning.[2] This is however no greater ontologising than saying that nothing, i.e. no form is admissible into the sphere of logic (in other words, can be said to have 'logical existence') unless it be in accordance with the laws

---

[1] This difference has been emphasized by Bar-Hillel, *loc. cit.* Some of the points made in this section may be taken as rejoinders to the censure of Husserl by Bar-Hillel.

[2] cp., e.g., *L.U.*, II, 1, pp. 330–2.

of pure syntax. Here, the question about existence is a purely *internal* one.

§ 20.   After having given a sketch of Husserl's idea of a pure logical grammar whose task is to separate the meaningful from the meaningless, we should now turn to *the second and the next higher stratum of formal logic*, i.e. *to the logic of non-contradiction*. The following table, constructed in accordance with the analysis in § 14 of the IV Investigations in the *Logische Untersuchungen*, would help us in appreciating this transition:

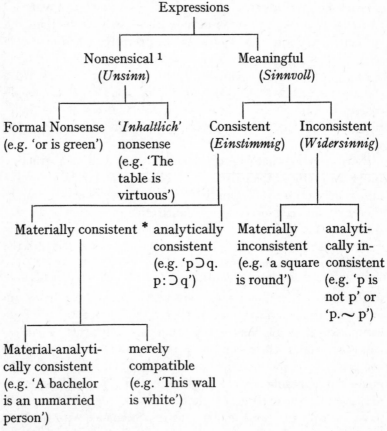

¹ The type of nonsense which pure logical grammar forbids has to be distinguished from another type of nonsense, often called by Husserl '*inhaltlich*' nonsense. The proposition 'The table is virtuous' e.g., is sanctioned by the laws of pure logical grammar, but owes its nonsensical character to the material incompatibility of what

If pure logical grammar is concerned with the distinction between the nonsensical and the meaningful [1] and lays down laws that guide this distinction, the formal logic of non-contradiction is concerned with the distinction between the consistent and the inconsistent, more specifically with the distinction between analytic consistency and analytic contradiction and lays down laws that guide that distinction. ('S is not S' is not nonsense but is analytically inconsistent.) The Law of contradiction is the supreme law of this part of formal logic. Husserl calls this logic of non-contradiction 'Pure apophantic Analytic.' To this domain belongs the entire formal theory of syllogism as well as formal mathematical analysis.[1] A full development of this domain leads to Leibniz's conception of a *mathesis universalis*.[2]

20.1.　From the very beginning of his logical investigations, Husserl was well aware of the basic unity of logic and mathematics, though he also never lost sight of their differences.[3] However, in spite of all his pronounced enthusiasm over mathematical logic, he never ceased to warn against identifying logic with the technique of mathematics. Logic as a philosophical science, he points out, raises questions which are beyond the narrow technical interest of the mathematician *qua* mathe-

has been called the *Kernstoffe*. The source of such incompatibility obviously falls outside the scope of logic (*F.u.t.L.*, p. 196).

　* This further division of material consistency is in accordance with the distinction between '*Konsequenz*' and mere compatibility (or empty noncontradiction) drawn in *F.u.t.L.*, p. 56. In the former case, the predicate is analytically contained in the subject. It is of course possible to suggest that 'The square has four sides' is analytically consistent and therefore should not be brought under the 'materially consistent.' I have however preferred this arrangement in view of the fact that in *L.U.*, II, 1, p. 335, Husserl mentions 'The square is round' as an example of material inconsistency. Analytic consistency and inconsistency should therefore be ascribed only to expressions in which no material word occurs, i.e. to purely symbolic expressions. I have therefore characterized 'The square is round' as a case of material inconsistency, but in order to indicate its fundamental difference from compatibility, I have coined the expression 'material-analytic consistency,' thereby differentiating it from pure, i.e. formal-analytic consistency.

　[1] *F.u.t.L.*, p. 48.
　[2] *ibid.*, p. 65.
　[3] In *L.U.*, I, pp. 219–220, he confesses that he has special sympathy for the "*Grösse der Mathematik und Logik in eins setzenden Konzeptionen.*" "*Die Geringschätzung, mit welcher die philosophischen Logiker über die mathematischen Theorien der Schlüsse zu sprechen lieben, ändert nichts daran, dass die mathematische Form der Behandlung bei diesen ... die einzig wissenschaftliche ist ....*" (p. 253). In *F.u.t.L.*, p. 70, he accuses the "philosophical logicians of modern times" of inability to grasp the significance of mathematical logic and of remaining confined within the limits of the Aristotelian-Scholastic tradition.

matician. Mere formal mathematics – the mathematics of the mathematicians [1] – is not the same as formal logic. In formal logic, the true *meaning* of formal mathematics receives clarification. He further tells us [2] that the true logical significance of formal mathematics runs the risk of losing itself in an increasing symbolism.

Aristotle no doubt founded formal logic by replacing the material words by variables like S, p, etc., but he could not arrive at the idea of pure form inasmuch as his logic remained directed towards the real world and contained much that was metaphysical.[3] It was through the extension of algebra to logic that the idea of pure form seems to have been developed, though Husserl gives the credit of an early discovery even to Duns Scotus.

Why is it then that the inner unity of logic and mathematics could not be appreciated by the ancients? Husserl adduces three "historical reasons" [4] for this:

First, the ancients did not develop the idea of pure logical form, just as in mathematics they had not isolated pure arithmetic from geometry and mechanics. Secondly, they had not learnt to abstract the proposition as an objective structure from the subjective act of judging. It required naturally much advance in philosophical thought to recognize the ideal-objectivity of the logical structures, this recognition being in no small measure hindered by the "*altererbte Ängste vor dem Platonismus.*" The recognition came first in mathematics, and only then of course in logic. Finally, the situation became vitiated by the psychologism that prevailed amongst philosophers of the last century.

To these three may be added a fourth consideration, i.e., the widely held view that logic is a normative science. This conception of logic as a normative science and of logical laws as normative laws was set up against psychologism and thus gained wide acceptance. But what it failed to appreciate is the fact that pure logic is a *theoretical* science, that its laws are theoretical – though not natural or psychological – laws,[5] and that though they are

---

[1] *F.u.t.L.*, p. 125.

[2] *F.u.t.L.*, § 33.

[3] *F.u.t.L.*, p. 43. Veatch's *Intentional Logic*, Yale, 1952, developed on Aristotelian lines, should not therefore be taken to be entirely in line with Husserl.

[4] *F.u.t.L.*, § 26.

[5] *L.U.*, I, p. 164–5.

not in themselves normative they might yet serve as norms.[1] In fact, every theoretical proposition might be made to serve as a norm. Conversely, underlying every normative proposition as its basis, there is a theoretical proposition.[2]

20.2. Be the "historical reasons" what they may, the conception of logic as a theoretical science and as the science of pure form has come to stay in our times. There is however another distinction which the Aristotelian-scholastic tradition had failed to develop. Husserl calls his second stratum of logic not only 'logic of non-contradiction' but also *'Konsequenzlogik.'* Traditional logic of non-contradiction with its normative attitude made use of the law of non-contradiction as a prohibitive principle: the task of this logic was *how to avoid* contradiction and how to formulate the formal laws necessary for this purpose. The idea of a logic of consistency in the sense of a formally 'compossible' system had not yet dawned upon the traditional logicians before Leibniz.

'Konsequenz' or 'consistency' may mean either bare compatibility, i.e., 'trivial non-contradiction' or analytic necessity.[3] The notion of compatibility goes beyond formal logic and has to find its rationale in the nature of reality. The question why two predicates are merely compatible while two others are not cannot admit of any *logical* answer: we are to fall back upon ontology. Formal logic of non-contradiction is a 'logic of consistency' only in the second sense of the term 'consistency.' Pure formal logic of non-contradiction is to be a compossible system of formal propositions held together by the relation of analytic necessity. In this strict sense of analytic compossibility, logic of non-contradiction is also a logical *system.* Thus we come to the idea of a deductive system which, according to Stebbing, is "a special kind of system in which the elements are propositions and the

---

[1] *ibid.*, p. 158. Also *F.u.t.L.*, p. 28: "*Die Logik wird normativ, wird praktisch, sie kann in entsprechender Änderung der Einstellung in eine normativ-technologische Disziplin umgewendet werden. Aber sie selbst ist an sich nicht normative Disziplin, sondern eben Wissenschaft im prägnanten Sinne ....*"

[2] *L.U.*, I, p. 48. For example, the normative proposition 'An A ought to be B' contains the theoretic proposition 'An A which is B has the further property C,' where C stands for a value-predicate like 'good'.

[3] *F.u.t.L.*, p. 291.

relations between elements are logical relations." [1] To such a system all questions of truth and falsity are extraneous: hence the distinction between 'logic of consistency' and 'logic of truth.' We should therefore have to look more carefully into this last distinction as drawn by Husserl. Before doing this, however, we have to pause to examine *Husserl's notion of analyticity.*

20.3. The notion of analyticity has figured prominently in contemporary philosophical discussions, and it must be said with all fairness that Husserl was not aware of all the difficulties that surround this issue. Quine has distinguished between two different cases of analyticity typified respectively by the two following examples:

      (1) 'No bachelor is married.'
      (2) 'No unmarried person is married.'

The analyticity of (1) presupposes the notion of synonymity and Quine, as is well known, would not accept it so long as a satisfactory criterion of synonymity has not been found out. (2) is analytic in a different sense, i.e., in the sense that it remains true whatever interpretation be put on the non-logical words of the sentence. In other words, in (2) only the logical words occur 'essentially' and all others occur 'vacuously.' Statements of the second type are, according to Quine, 'logically true.' [The statement (1) can of course be transformed into a logical truth "by putting synonyms for synonyms," [2] but this presupposes synonymity which is what distinguishes it from the case (2).]

It should be clear that the notion of analyticity which Quine suspects and finally rejects might be characterized as that of *material*-analyticity, as contrasted with that of *formal*-analyticity. Husserl is well aware of this distinction. In the 3rd Investigations of the *Logische Untersuchungen* Vol. II, he draws a distinction between 'analytic laws' ('*analytische Gesetze*') and 'analytic Necessities' ('*analytische Notwendigkeiten*'). "Analytic laws," we are told,[3] "are unconditionally universal propositions (and are therefore free from all explicit or implicit assertion of the existence of individuals) which contain no other concepts

---

[1] L. S. Stebbing, *A Modern Introduction to Logic*, London, 1946, 5th edition, p. 174.
[2] Quine, *From a Logical Point of View*, Harvard, 1953, p. 23.
[3] *L.U.*, II, 1, p. 254.

except the formal ones, and – if we go back to the primitive ones – which therefore contain none other than the formal categories." To be contrasted with such analytic laws are their 'specifications' (*Besonderungen*) which "arise through the introduction of material concepts and possibly of concepts that posit individual existence (e.g., 'this, 'the king')." [1] Husserl now goes on to tell us that just as in all cases specifications of laws yield us 'necessities' so also here specifications of analytic 'laws' yield us analytic 'necessities.' A further terminological remark is added that it is these analytic 'necessities' that are to be called analytic 'propositions' (*Sätze*). Accordingly, 'analytically necessary propositions' are defined as "propositions whose truth is fully independent of the matter of fact peculiarity of their objectivities (whether thought as determinate, or in indeterminate generality) and of the possible facthood of the cases, i.e., of the validity of the possible existential positing." They are, for that reason, also propositions "that allow themselves to be fully *formalized* and be apprehended as specifications or empirical applications of the formal or analytical laws that have validly arisen through such process of formalization." [2] The examples which Husserl gives of such analytically necessary propositions are: 'There cannot be a king without there being subjects,' 'The existence of this house includes the existence of its walls and other parts,' and 'If this house is red, Redness belongs to it.'

Now it might safely be presumed that under 'analytically necessary propositions,' Husserl includes both the types of analytic propositions mentioned above. For, in both cases we have replaced empty variables by material non-logical words; both might be viewed as empirical specifications of analytic 'laws.' The very important difference between them which has been brought out by Quine has escaped Husserl's notice, for he does not quite see that in 'No unmarried person is married' the non-logical word 'married,' is used vacuously (in the sense that the truth value of the proposition is independent of any in-

---

[1] *ibid.*, p. 255.

[2] *L.U.*, II, 1, p. 255. Husserl is well aware (cp. *ibid.*, p. 256 fn. 1) that this definition of analyticity is a more satisfactory one than that of Kant. The credit for having first made this improvement over Kant goes therefore to Husserl. The various definitions suggested by Carnap, Church and Quine and Waismann more or less follow Husserl's pattern.

terpretation that might be given to it). The distinction between
the two cases owes its importance however to the fact that it
serves to focus attention on the really philosophical problem
about material-analyticity.

Material-analyticity is definable by appealing (i) either to a
realm of meanings (Lewis, Husserl), or (ii) to linguistic definition
(Waismann), or (iii) to an artificial language with its 'semantical
rules' (Carnap). Some others reduce such analyticity to the
contrary-to-fact conditional, not knowing that the latter offers
"a very sandy foundation." [1] Quine demands a behaviouristic
criterion and, not finding one, rejects, in company with Goodman, all material-analyticity. Thus concludes Goodman: "no
non-repetitive statement will be analytic. The most we can say is
that it is more or less, nearly analytic. [2]

So far as formal logic is concerned – it must be said at once –
Husserl's reliance on the notion of analyticity is not in any way
affected by the apparent dubiousness of the notion of material-
analyticity. Nevertheless, it is necessary to lay down what can
be said with regard to this latter notion from the standpoint of
Husserl's philosophy:

If there is any point in the recent criticisms of the notion of
material-analyticity, it is not that we do not know or cannot
know whether a given non-logical proposition is analytic, but
that we cannot adduce a sufficient criterion of synonymity. As
one critic has pointed out, [3] the difficulty is inherent in any question
about the criteria of sameness. To explain what synonymity or
bare sameness is, is impossible, for any such explanation presupposes one's capacity to recognize synonymity or sameness.
The idea of sameness of meaning is too fundamental to be explained by any notion other than itself. To deny synonymity,
as Goodman does, [4] just because a satisfactory criterion is not
forthcoming, is to distort, even to deny, phenomena for the sake
of saving rational theory – a procedure which is contrary to the
spirit of a phenomenological philosophy.

---

[1] M. White, "The Analytic and the Synthetic," (in Linsky, *loc. cit.*, p. 284).

[2] N. Goodman, "On Likeness of Meaning," (in Linsky, *loc. cit.*, p. 74).

[3] R. Taylor, "Disputes about synonymy," *The Philosophical Review*, 1954, pp. 517–529.

[4] N. Goodman, *loc. cit.*: "no two different words have the same meaning," p. 73.

20.4. Husserl defines the formal logic of non-contradiction or the 'logic of consistency' by the notion of analyticity.[1] Some recent opinions on such a definition need to be taken into consideration.

Quine in his article on Strawson's Logic [2] rejects the definition of logic with the help of terms like 'analytic' and prefers to define the scope of logic with the notions of truth and logical vocabulary: "the business of formal logic is describable as that of finding statement forms which are *logical*, in the sense of containing no constants beyond the logical vocabulary, and (extensionally) *valid*, in the sense that all statements exemplifying the form in question are true." [3] To this definition of formal logic Husserl would have objected by pointing out that it makes use of the notion of *truth* which, as we shall see, belongs to the next stratum of logical enquiry. Pure logic of non-contradiction, Husserl would say, is free from the notion of truth and so need not be defined with its help.

This comment also reflects Husserl's attitude towards the modern conception of formal logic as being tautologous in character.[4] Becker has shown that the word 'Tautology' has different meanings in logic of non-contradiction and in logic of truth. Following Becker, we might say that:

(i) in logic of non-contradiction, P is a tautology if and when P is consistent with both p_1 and not-p_1, with both p_2 and not-p_2.., with both p_n and not-p_n;

Whereas (ii) in logic of truth, P is a tautology if the truth value of P (p_1, p_2....p_n) remains the same if p_1 is replaced by not-p_1, p_2 by not-p_2... and p_n by not-p_n.

This shows that Wittgenstein's definition of tautology in terms of truth-function belongs to the Logic of Truth, and should be avoided in a pure logic of non-contradiction.

[1] In *Beilage* III, § 3 to *F.u.t.L.*, Husserl approves of another notion of analyticity besides the fundamental definition given in the *Logische Untersuchungen*. Formal Logic of non-contradiction, he tells us, is *also* analytic in the Kantian sense of '*blossen Erkenntniserläuterung*' as against an '*Erkenntniserweiterung.*' "The analytic interest," he goes on to say, "is directed simply towards the possibility of clarificatory-evidence" (p. 295).

[2] W. V. O. Quine, "Mr. Strawson on Logical Theory," *Mind*, 1953, pp. 433–451.

[3] *ibid.*, p. 436.

[4] Fortunately, *Formale und transzendentale Logik* contains with Husserl's approval an Appendix by O. Becker on "*Bemerkungen über Tautologie im Sinne der Logistik*" (*Beilage* III, § 4).

But it should be clearly remembered that though the character of being tautologous may be ascribed (in two different senses, as we have just seen) to the two higher strata of logical enquiry, we can by no means extend the same characterization to the primary stratum of logical grammar or pure syntax.

20.5.   The above discussion has further brought it to light that the exact nature of Husserl's notion of a pure logic of non-contradiction cannot be understood except by contrasting it with his own notion of a logic of truth. Husserl has claimed that his distinction is something quite new.[1] The distinction, if it was at all drawn before, *was* nothing other than the distinction between a formal-logical inquiry that disregards all content of knowledge and a logic that takes into consideration all such material content. In that sense, a logic of truth would be a metaphysical logic discussing questions like: how can we have true knowledge of the real world? etc.

This is not what Husserl means by a logic of truth. His logic of truth does *not* go beyond formal logic: it constitutes rather the third and in a sense the final stratum of formal logic. It is not a metaphysical or philosophical logic in the traditional Kantian-Hegelian sense. Even modern symbolic logic, Husserl could have said, has failed to draw this distinction: as is evident from Wittgenstein's definition of tautology and from Quine's definition of the scope of formal logic.

A logic of truth has to enquire into "the formal laws of possible truth." [2] And yet it shall remain confined "to the mere forms of judgments." How can such a formal logic, it may be asked, become also a logic of *truth*? Is it possible to acquire 'essential insight' into the *formal* nature of possible truth of judgments? [3] The pure logic of non-contradiction is of course a necessary but not a sufficient condition of the possibility of truth. To be able to appreciate the distinction between the two strata of logical enquiry, therefore, it would be useful to see how the law of non-contradiction receives two different formulations in the two cases.[4]

---

[1] *F.u.t.L.*, p. 63. He calls it *"ein grundwesentlich Neues"* even if it is *"den Worten nach allbekannt."*

[2] *F.u.t.L.*, § 15.

[3] *ibid.*, p. 58.

[4] For these formulations, *F.u.t.L.*, § 20.

(i) In logic of non-contradiction, the principle should be formulated thus: 'Of two contradictory judgments, p and ∼p, not both can be brought to 'clarificatory evidence,' not both have ideal 'mathematical existence'.' This principle may also be objectively formulated free from the subjective language of 'clarificatory evidence.' An objective statement of the principle would be: 'Every contradictory judgment is 'excluded' by the judgment which it contradicts. Every judgment which is an analytic consequence of another judgment is 'included' within it.' [1]

(ii) The more usual formulation belongs to the logic of truth: 'If a judgment p is true, its contradictory ∼p is false.'

The distinction between the two logics may be further clarified by taking up the traditional forms of *modus ponens* (and *tollens*) and by showing how this basic logical form fares in the two.

(i) In logic of non-contradiction, it should be formulated thus: 'From two judgments of the form 'If M, then N' and 'M,' it follows analytically that 'N.' Similarly, from two judgments of the form 'If M, then N' and 'not-N,' it follows analytically that 'not-M.'

(ii) In logic of truth, the principle runs thus: 'If the antecedent of a hypothetical judgment is true, it follows that the consequence is true. If the consequence is false, the antecedent is false.' Or, 'If it is true both that 'If M, then N' and that 'M,' then 'N, is also true.' If it is true both that 'If M, then N' and that 'not-N,' then 'not-M' is also true.'

It is clear then that the pure logic of non-contradiction does not admit of the predicates 'true' and 'false.' All its laws have to be formulated without introducing these semantical predicates. It also seems to be obvious that what Husserl calls the logic of truth is not an entirely new discipline which he either constructs or for whose construction he suggests the ground plan.[2] Formal Logic has remained both, a logic of non-contradiction as well as a logic of truth in Husserl's sense. What Husserl is trying to do is to separate these two aspects and to suggest the possibility of a pure logic of non-contradiction in which 'true' and 'false' would not appear and a pure logic of truth which would be specially concerned with the formal laws guiding these two

---

[1] *ibid.*, p. 168.
[2] It is therefore not quite the same as the modern formal semantics.

semantical predicates. The conception of truth-value introduced by Frege and developed by Wittgenstein would belong to the latter logic. It is further possible to render every law of the pure logic of non-contradiction into a law of the logic of truth, and vice versa. Thus the two logics should appear to be two alternative possibilities rather than two *strata*, one built upon the other. Yet there is some justification for Husserl's conception of 'strata' inasmuch as the notion of non-contradiction is logically prior to the notion of truth and forms its indispensable pre-condition.

We are however yet to come to the *really fundamental point of distinction* between the two logics and between their attitudes. The 'subjective' formulation of the law of non-contradiction in pure logic of non-contradiction speaks of 'clarificatory evidence.' Husserl also says: not both of two contradictory judgments are, as genuine ('*eigentliche*') judgments, possible. What is the significance of all this?

We have used the word 'judgment' in all three cases: the pure logical grammar, the pure logic of non-contradiction and the pure logic of truth, all these three are concerned with judgments. But the notion of judgment is not quite the same in all these contexts. Logic of truth alone, of all three, is concerned with *actual* judgments (in other words, with assertions). The other two are concerned with *possible* judgments, the meaning of 'possibility' being different in each of them. Pure logical grammar is concerned with possible judgments in the widest sense of 'possible'; pure logic of non-contradiction is concerned with possible judgments in a somewhat narrower sense of 'possible.' It would be more in the fitness of things to reserve the word 'judgment' only for logic of truth, and to use the word 'proposition' for the first two strata. It remains to be explained what are the two relevant senses of 'possibility.'

For pure logical grammar a proposition is possible in so far as it is merely meant or understood. In this widest sense, even the self-contradictory proposition 'S is not S' is a possible one: 'possibility' here is equivalent to 'accordance with the laws of syntax.' But all propositions that are possible in this sense are not capable of being 'clarified.' In pure logic of non-contradiction, a proposition is accepted as 'possible,' i.e. as a genuine proposition only if it is free from contradiction; in this logic considered as a 'consistent system,' a proposition is admissible if it is 'compossible.' (It is only in this sense that Husserl speaks of a proposition as having ideal existence). Again, not all propositions that are so possible actually asserted.[1] When a proposition is not merely understood with clarity but actually asserted, it comes to acquire the properties of truth and falsity.

Truth and falsity are properties of asserted propositions, i.e., of actual judgments and *not* of propositions as such.[2] It is this important fact which makes it possible to distinguish a pure logic of non-contradiction from a logic of truth.[3]

It is the implicit presupposition of a logic of truth, Husserl goes on to tell us,[4] that every 'clear' (i.e. free from self-contradiction) judgment is *decidable* with regard to its truth and falsity. This presupposition entails another, logically prior one: that every judgment is in itself *decided*. This presupposition needs critical examination.

Husserl has two comments to offer so far as this question of decidability is concerned: first, he refers to the "immeasurable realm of occasional judgments" whose meaning and truth are determined by the *"typisch Gleichartigkeit der Situationen."* All questions about their decidability fall outside the scope of formal logic. Secondly, the law of excluded middle – and hence the assumption regarding decidability – does not hold good of *'inhaltlich'* non-sensical propositions [5] like 'Virtue is green.' It must however be remembered that these two comments are not to be taken as criticisms of the logical principles, for these two groups of judgments obviously do not fall within the formal logician's area of interest.

20.6.   The final step in the development of formal logic [6] is the construction of a pure deductive *Mannigfaltigkeitslehre.*

[1] *F.u.t.L.*, p. 62. *"In der Verworrenheit ist jedes Urteil möglich, das in der Deutlichkeit unmöglich ist, und in der Deutlichkeit wieder ist jedes Urteil möglich, das als einsichtige Erkenntnis unmöglich ist."*

[2] *F.u.t.L.*, p. 58; also see § 79.

[3] The distinction may also be connected with the way the modern logicians have sought to distinguish between implication and inference, so that inference may be said to belong to the logic of truth and implication to logic of non-contradiction. The logic of truth should also include (*F.u.t.L.*, p. 88 f) the logic of modality, i.e. the logic of the modal transformations of the notion of truth.

[4] *F.u.t.L.*, § 79.

[5] *ibid.*, § 90.

[6] *F.u.t.L.*, 28. Husserl, however, never calls it the fourth stratum, for in a sense the *Mannigfaltigkeitslehre* is to contain and comprehend the pure logic of non-contradiction

The construction of such a deductive *Mannigfaltigkeitslehre*, we are told, is necessitated by the new type of mathematical analysis made possible by the "revolutionary theoretical-technical development in the 19th century."

What is this new type of mathematics referred to by Husserl? "Pure mathematics, in the modern view," writes Hermann Weyl, "amounts to a general hypothetico-deductive theory of relations; it develops the theory of logical molds, without binding itself to the one or the other among the possible concrete interpretations."[1] Its objects are not numbers, but as Hankel puts it,[2] 'intellectual objects' independent of any concrete interpretation. The best fulfilment of this idea is to be found in the modern developments of Abstract Algebra as a most general deductive theory of formal structures so that the other branches of mathematics are capable of being exhibited as various interpretations of it.

It is on the pattern of this new mathematical theory that Husserl develops his conception of a *Mannigfaltigkeitslehre*, first in the *Logische Untersuchungen* Vol. I [3] and later in the *Formale und transzendentale Logik*.[4] Formal Logic should be a science of the conditions of the possibility of theory in general. Such a science however cannot but be an apriori theory of the various possible forms of theories.[5] All these various forms of theories again are not mutually unrelated but themselves constitute a system. Hence, it must be possible to construct a form of these forms, a *theory-form* whose 'interpretations' shall

and the logic of truth within its fold. When therefore Husserl calls the construction of a *Mannigfaltigkeitslehre* the "third and the highest task" of formal logic (*ibid.*, p. 78) he must be taken as referring to the other two aspects of formal logic, i.e. to formal apophantic and formal ontology, a distinction which would be treated in the next section of this chapter.

[1] Herman Weyl, *Philosophy of Mathematics and Natural Science*, Princeton, 1949, p. 27. For the method of constructing such a mold, see Weyl, p. 25, and Tarski, *Introduction to Logic*, New York, 1941, Ch. VI.

[2] In his *Theory of Complex Number* quoted by Weyl, *loc. cit.*

[3] §§ 69–70.

[4] §§ 28–35.

[5] A theory, according to Husserl (*L.U.*, I, pp. 236–7), must be, in order to be a theory in the strict sense, deductive in form. A theory is *"eine systematische Verknüp-fung von Sätzen in der Form einer systematisch einheitlichen Deduktion"* (*F.u.t.L.* pp. 78–9). Every theory can be considered as a 'theoretical totality.' All such sciences are called by Husserl 'nomological' and are sharply distinguished from the other sciences like psychology, phenomenology or history (*F.u.t.L.*, p. 89). The latter sciences do not permit formalization. Examples of nomological sciences are: pure mechanics, geometry, arithmetic etc. The 'system-form' of the non-nomological sciences is not formal-analytic. They cannot be reduced to the deductive form.

be all actual theories or from which other theories are 'deducible.' It must therefore be a theory of the utmost generality. The *Mannigfaltigkeitslehre* is now said to be 'the objective correlate'[1] of such a generalized theory-form. The objects of such a theory-form should be *Denkobjekten*, i.e. intellectual objects that are "fully undetermined with regard to their content," and are "neither individual nor specific singularities" and that are made definite exclusively through the form of the basic operations of the system. Nor are the basic operations any more determined with regard to their content; [2] they are made definite exclusively through the basic postulates. Husserl goes on to tell us that this represents a point of view without which one cannot speak of understanding the method of mathematics. [3]

Such a *Mannigfaltigkeitslehre* should bring formal logic to a completion: Husserl does not pursue what he calls in this connection the '*Ganzheitsprobleme*' [4] of logic to its final clarification. Similarly, he is aware of the problems of completeness (*Vollständigkeit*) and decision.[5] He defines a definite *Mannigfaltigkeit* with the help of the idea of completeness: its system of axioms must be such that every proposition (or propositional form) in it must be capable of being proved either 'true' (i.e., an analytic consequence of the axioms) or 'false' (i.e. an analytic contradiction).[6] This raises the question: how to prove a priori that a certain deductive theory is 'complete' in this sense or not, that every proposition in it is decidable? Husserl does not seem to have quite appreciated the difficulties connected with the decision problem which were later on brought to light by Tarski, Gödel and Church. On the other hand, he seems to be hopeful that completeness can be assured by supplementing the system of axioms of a theory – in the manner of Hilbert – by a set of 'axioms of completeness.' But it has been conclusively shown

---

[1] *L.U.*, I, p. 248.

[2] e.g. in the *Mannigfaltigkeitslehre*, the sign ' + ' does not signify addition of numbers but is defined exclusively by the laws like those of associativity, transitivity, commutativity etc.

[3] *L.U.*, I, p. 250.

[4] *F.u.t.L.*, p. 88.

[5] For the nature of these problems in deductive theories, see Tarski, *loc. cit.*, pp. 134–8.

[6] *F.u.t.L.*, p. 84. This definition of *Vollständigkeit* combines Tarski's ideas of consistency and completeness between which Husserl does not quite distinguish.

now by various investigators that arithmetic and advanced geometry are incomplete and do not admit of decidability.

A *Mannigfaltigkeitslehre*, Husserl adds, is not to be understood as a mere play with symbols but must necessarily have an ontological significance. In other words, instead of talking about signs and their permissible modes of composition, we must have to talk about the objects – even if 'intellectual' or abstract objects – and the laws of their combination.

20.7.   It is one of the standing reproaches against Husserl's philosophy of logic that he inevitably 'ontologises' and postulates a realm of meanings for ensuring the objectivity of logic. Some even go to the extent of ignorantly ascribing to him the view that formal logic involves synthetic a priori propositions. This last charge is inexcusably wrong. As to the general charge of ontologising, we could only say that Husserl no doubt ontologises but in a manner which hardly impairs the formal-analytic character of logic. In fact, the peculiarity of his philosophy of logic is that he recognizes its many facets and seeks to integrate them into one *disjunctive* whole. For what he insists on is the possibility of taking up different attitudes, three of which dominate his studies. It is possible, to start with, to take up a formal-apophantic attitude which yields a formal logic of propositional forms. But it is also possible to switch over to an ontological attitude which would 'transform' the formal logic to a formal ontology.[1] A third possibility lies in the subjective direction, yielding what Husserl calls *'transcendental'* logic.

Every ontology is concerned with a region of objects. Formal ontology however has for its region the 'empty' formal region which, strictly speaking, is not another region besides the others but the 'empty form of region in general.' [2] It may also be called the 'empty' region of object-in-general.[3] Its categories are said to be 'categorial modifications' of object-in-general; its objects are the socalled 'categorial objects' like unity, plu-

---

[1] *F.u.t.L.*, p. 131. cp. *Ideen*, p. 362: (In this changed attitude,) instead of 'propositions' one now speaks of 'states of affair,' instead of 'propositional constituents' one speaks of objectivities, instead of 'predicative meanings' one speaks of 'properties.' One also talks no more about the truth or validity of propositions, but about the subsistence of 'states of affair,' about the being of objects etc.

[2] *Ideen*, p. 27.

[3] *F.u.t.L.*, p. 132.

rality, relation, property and sets. 'Numbers' of traditional mathematics are also such 'categorial' objects.[1] In *Erfahrung und Urteil* [2] Husserl calls them *'Verstandesgegenständlichkeiten'* and shows how they have their 'origin' in predicative thought.

We have thus completed the picture of formal logic that Husserl has to offer us. In this account we have of course left out one major aspect of Husserl's philosophy of logic, i.e. his transcendental logic. The picture that he offers us is a stratified one: the pure logical grammar at the base, a pure logic of non-contradiction in the middle, and a pure logic of truth on the top. But there is finally a pure *Mannigfaltigkeitslehre* which gives us a pure form of all deductive theories to crown the progress of formal logical investigations. Side by side there is the possibility of switching off to an objective, ontological attitude which leads to a formal ontology of the 'empty' region of object-in-general.[3]

At one place,[4] Husserl tells us that his task is to give a systematic clarification of 'the teleological structure of the Idea of logic,' to illuminate the idea of logic in accordance with its 'immanent teleological structure.' I think what he means by this 'teleological structure' is nothing but this inner stratification – dynamically conceived, i.e., this process of inner development – of formal logic.[5]

While recognizing the purity, the apriority and the analyticity of formal logic, Husserl nevertheless investigates into its 'origin.' In his *Prolegomena,* he has once for ever rejected psychologism.

---

[1] Husserl distinguishes in *F.u.t.L.*, § 24, between 'apophantic mathematics' which permits itself to be reduced into propositional logic and 'non-apophantic mathematics' which does not so permit itself and by which he means the traditional mathematics of numbers, sets, combinations and permutations etc. The concept of number, it follows, is equivocal.

[2] pp. 282 ff.

[3] We find in C.S. Peirce a similar – though not quite the same – threefold division of the province of logic. Peirce's three parts of logic are: (i) pure grammar which is "the doctrine of the general conditions of symbols and other signs having the significant character"; (ii) logic proper which is "the formal science of the conditions of the truth of representations"; and (iii) pure rhetoric, which studies the formal conditions of the force of symbols to appeal to a mind. (Buchler, *Philosophical Writings of C.S. Peirce*, New York, 1955, pp. 99 and 379).

[4] *F.u.t.L.*, p. 66.

[5] At other places, e.g. in *F.u.t.L.*, p. 182, Husserl regards it, as it were, an immanent end of logic to serve the purpose of the concrete sciences and to be applicable to the individuals of primary experience. For his concept of experience, see the following chapter.

Now that the objectivity of the logical is assured, a fresh enquiry into its 'origin' is not regarded any more to be misleading.

About this question of 'origin' of the logical, Husserl, it seems, has two *types* of answers. At first, there is an attempt, through a subjectively oriented enquiry, to trace the logical forms and objectivities to the subjective 'evidence' in which they are 'given.' In this context, Husserl speaks of the 'production' of the logical objectivities in consciousness. But he warns us [1] explicitly enough so as to remove all further chances of misunderstanding, that 'production' here does not mean what ordinarily it means when we say e.g. 'The carpenter has produced a book case.' As to what positively 'production' means, he goes on to tell us that 'producing' is here the same as 'making evident': *'erzeugen'* = *'darbieten.'* The consciousness in which the logical idealities are 'produced' is nothing other than *"diese evident machende Bewusstseins-tätigkeit."* To enquire therefore into the 'original modes of givenness' of the different logical objectivities is *not* to reduce the latter into mental states, but it is to establish a correlation, to discover the intentionality, between the mode of consciousness that presents and the objectivity that is presented through it.

There are three different attitudes in philosophizing: the ontological or the material, the linguistic or the formal, the phenomenological or the subjective. What Husserl intends to do is to establish the unity, by showing their correlation, of these three modes. If he has succeeded in this task, this may be regarded as the source of his singular relevance in the present, highly bewildering philosophical situation.

The second answer, suggested in the *Formale und transzendentale Logik* but explicitly developed in the later works, chiefly in the *Krisis* and the *Erfahrung und Urteil*, is this: all meanings, all idealities including the logico-mathematical ones have their 'origin' in the universal basis of pre-predicative experience.

The two answers are not mutually incompatible. It is only in the latter case that one could speak of 'origin' in the true sense: not only do the various sciences develop *temporally* out of this universal basis of pre-predicative experience, they are based on it, are supported by it, and always refer back to it. When however

[1] *F.u.t.L.*, § 63.

the idealities are 'traced' to their constitution in transcendental consciousness, what is meant, as we have seen, is that they are given through definite modes of consciousness, or that it is in definite modes of consciousness that we are to look for the evidence for definite types of objectivities.

In our last chapter, we shall now turn to this universal basis of pre-predicative experience.

CHAPTER VII

BACK TO EXPERIENCE

§ 22. Formal logic replaces the material words by logical variables. If material words do occur in a statement of formal logic, they occur only vacuously. Within formal logic, therefore, an appeal to *experience* (in the sense to be specified below) is not called for. [In the construction of a formal system, the only sense in which an appeal to intuition *may* be permitted would be through the process of construction: it is in this sense that the intuitionists oppose the so-called formalists in philosophy of mathematics.] Formal logic has, as a consequence, a claim to autonomy. This claim is certainly justified to a certain extent, especially inasmuch as no empirical consideration weighs in matters concerning any decision within the system. But the claim to autonomy, when made absolute, results in a naivity which should be exposed.[1] Such naivity shows itself in the conception of logic as a mere play with symbols against which Husserl spares no opportunity to combat. Just as one of the tasks of a *philosophy* of logic is to exhibit the immanent teleology of logical thought by showing its inner stratifications leading up to a *mathesis universalis*, similarly another of its tasks is to expose the limitations of the claim of formal logic to autonomy, by tracing it back to its origin in pre-predicative experience. The sense in which pre-predicative experience provides the foundation for formal logic is totally different from the sense in which a pure logical syntax constitutes its basic stratum. Syntax constitutes the lowest stratum *within* formal logic; but it also always points back towards the pre-logical. As soon as, by analysis, we come to the notion of '*Kernstoff*' (as distinguished from '*Kernform*'),[2] we are on the furthest lower limit of the

[1] *Krisis*, p. 144.
[2] See § 19.5 above.

logical. This limit could be brought out in another way, as mentioned earlier in connection with what has been called 'material (*inhaltlich*) nonsense': though formal nonsense is accounted for by the rules of logical grammar, material nonsense owes its origin to incompatibilities rooted in the *de facto* nature of our experience.

22.1.   The argument by which, in *Formale und transzendentale Logik*, predicative thought in general (and not merely formal logic) is traced back to experience is as follows.[1] There is a sense in which the logically most primitive judgments may be said to be the *individual* judgments. Individuals again are given through experience in the original and also most significant sense of the term. The individual judgments may therefore be called 'empirical judgments' (*Erfahrungsurteile*). Thus, starting from the higher levels of predicative judgments and coming down regressively to lower levels we ultimately reach the individual or empirical judgments. But likewise we might start with the individual judgments and with the twofold processes of material and formal generalizations [2] rise up to higher levels of concrete predicative thought on the one hand and formal logic on the other. The argument is very much Russellian and one wonders if Husserl's individual judgments are very different from Russell's basic propositions. Unfortunately, Husserl does not give any good example of his individual judgments, and so we cannot say whether they should necessarily be ego-centric in character. Russell's basic propositions are not, as is now well known, all that simple and unanalysable and non-descriptive which Russell intended them to be. Husserl also does not unambiguously tell us whether he intends his individual judgments to be taken as being pre-predicative. If he so intended, then he would be wrong. The individual judgment is still judgment, and therefore also predicative. In *Erfahrung und Urteil*, Husserl practically admits this: he tells us there [3] that there is a certain degree of idealization even in the so-called judgments of experience, at least in so far as we use common names for the individual objects given

[1] *F.u.t.L.*, § 84.
[2] *ibid.*, § 87.
[3] *E.u.U.*, p. 58.

in experience.[1] This is something which Russell did not clearly see in connection with his basic propositions. But the distinction between Russell's basic propositions and Husserl's judgments of experience would in the long run be traced back to their different conceptions of what is given in pre-predicative experience, a question to which we shall turn in one of the following sections.

With regard to formal logic, the *Erfahrung und Urteil* argues its origin from experience in a rather slightly different form. Anything and everything, even the higher categorial objectivities, can be the *substrate* of a judgment. The *substrate* of a judgment is also called the *'Gegenstand-Worüber,'* i.e., the object *about* which the judgment is being made. Now, since any and every object, simple or complex, primary or categorial, can function in that capacity, formal logic proceeds to replace the concrete substrate by x: this suffices for the purposes of formal logic. But once we enquire into what could possibly be substituted for x, we come to ontology: what could be substituted must have possible being.[2] Logic in this sense is said to be mundane.[3] The actually given world no doubt stays in the background. It might even be claimed that logic pertains to an a priori possible world. But the possible world is a modal transformation of the actual.[4] Of all such possible judgmental *substrates* (or, *Gegenstände-Worüber*) the more complex ones are to be traced back to the simple ones, the categorial ones to the primary ones. These simple and primary objects called 'individuals' are also called the 'last substrates.' 'Experience' is *defined* in terms of these. In Russell's language, it might be suggested that whereas the more complex objects and the categorial ones are merely *Gegenstände-Worüber*, *about* which one can judge, the simple, primary individuals are so in the more specific sense of being *constituents* of the judgments concerned.[5] This, however, is not quite true. For, as Stebbing tells us, Russell is using 'constituent' in such a sense "that a given object, A, cannot be said to be a constituent of a given

---

[1] He does not undertake to discuss the large problem of the relation between expression and predicative thinking. cp. *E.u.U.*, p. 234.

[2] *ibid.*, p. 36.

[3] *ibid.*, p. 37.

[4] *F.u.t.L.*, p. 199.

[5] See Stebbing's distinction between two meanings of 'about' in this connection in *A Modern Introduction to Logic*, 5th edition, p. 34.

proposition p, unless it would be logically impossible that p should be asserted, or believed, or considered at all if there were no such object as A." [1] Husserl would not quite agree with this. For Russell's notion implies a theory of proper names and an atomism which would not be acceptable to him.[2] Further, even when a *Sachverhalt* is asserted, there is some sense in which the *Sachverhalt* asserted must subsist as a categorial object. Again, there is also a very important sense in which neither the individual substrate nor the *Sachverhalt* could be said to be a 'constituent' of the judgment concerned; and this is so in the sense that no real thing, event or *Sachverhalt* could be totally, i.e. *adäquat* given in any judgment.[3]

22.2. What the *Erfahrung und Urteil* does in the case of logic, the *Krisis* does in connection with mathematics, especially geometry and the natural sciences.

The *Krisis*, as its title suggests, starts with the idea of a crisis which modern science is regarded as facing. Examination of this crisis, its historical origin and its future leads to the question of the *foundation* of the sciences. Only one aspect of this crisis interests us here, and it is this: Husserl is very much concerned with the growing technological and symbolical character, and the consequent *Sinnentleerung*, of the natural sciences. We have seen in the foregoing chapter that Husserl, even in his early works, and in spite of his great admiration for mathematical logic, never ceased to suspect the mere play with symbols, the mere technique with which many professionals are apt to confuse the true nature of logic and mathematics. This suspicion comes to the forefront in the *Krisis*.[4] Broadly speaking, Husserl comes to believe that the natural sciences as well as geometry were, in their origin, far closer to experience than they are at present, and used to derive their truth-value from their function in experience. (Geometry, to take the familiar case for illustration, originally developed out of the need for measuring fields.) Formalisation of mathematics is no doubt both justified and necessary, but we must *not forget* the basis from which it all

---

[1] L. S. Stebbing, *loc. cit.*, p. 154.
[2] See § 17 above.
[3] *E.u.U.*, pp. 346–7.
[4] *Krisis*, pp. 45–8.

sprang. This forgetfulness of the *Sinnesfundament* is, we are told, in a large measure due to Galileo's attempt to give a purely quantitative-mathematical account of all nature, including the qualitative fulness of sensible contents. The mathematicization of the sense qualities, though indirectly led to what Whitehead calls 'bifurcation of nature' into a real core consisting of mathematical forms and an appearance consisting of qualitative contents. Sensible experience, considered as *doxa*, was now finally subordinated to mathematical reason whose autonomy was fully assured thereby. Husserl protests against this bifurcation as fully as Whitehead did, and aims at restoring to *doxa* its rightful place as the basis, the foundation, as well as the standing support of that reason.[1] This forgotten *Sinnesfundament* is nothing other than the so-called *Lebenswelt*. The sciences (or *Episteme* in general) are regarded by Husserl as a sort of transformation (in the sense of idealization) of this *Lebenswelt*, into whose structure we should therefore enquire. The crisis of the sciences consists in self-forgetfulness; the remedy suggested is the attainment of self-knowledge.

22.3. If this were all that is needed, Husserl's contention would, in a large measure, pass unchallenged. For few would like to controvert the claim that the natural sciences, even the most mathematical of them, and mathematics itself, originated from the needs and practices of experience. However, in the course of their development they have become theoretical enquiries. It is right therefore that this fact about their origin be kept in mind. But what could be the significance of this appeal to *Lebenswelt*, except that it reminds the scientists of something they are likely to forget? Does Husserl want to recommend a change in the structure of the sciences themselves? Does he mean to suggest that the sciences should cease to be formal and symbolic? Now, it goes without saying that such a proposal would be preposterous. *Nor does Husserl anywhere put forward such a proposal.* It is not one of the tasks of philosophers to recommend to the scientists anything affecting their method or subject-matter. All that Husserl seems to be saying is that a proper *philosophical* understanding of the sciences should take

[1] cp. *E.u.U.*, pp. 22; 44.

into consideration the close and inseparable connection which they have with experience.

Regarding predicative thought in general and logic in particular, Husserl puts forward *a more far-reaching, and therefore a more controversial thesis*. He seems to maintain the view that even in pre-predicative immediate experience there are given features which may be regarded as the *origin* of predicative and logical thinking. He tells us in the *Erfahrung und Urteil* that the realm of the logical is far wider in scope than what has been handled by traditional logic and proposes to trace the logical structures back to their lowest strata in pre-predicative experience (whereas traditional logic, in that case, must be supposed to begin at a much higher level)[1]

More specifically speaking, he undertakes upon himself the tasks of exhibiting:

(i) that each of the different forms of judgment, discussed in formal logic, originates in some feature of pre-predicative experience;

(ii) that induction and scientific inference, as processes of thinking, originate in an ubiquitous characteristic of the most primitive experience;

and (iii) finally, that the universals of thought have their origin in the *typicality* that characterizes pre-predicative experience.

The *Erfahrung und Urteil* is mainly devoted to the first task, while both the *Krisis* and the *Erfahrung und Urteil* develop the other two themes. Our purpose here is not to go into the details of Husserl's expositions, but to bring out only those of his arguments that would help us in making a final appraisal of his resulting philosophy of thought. To show whatever little is relevant for our limited purpose would require however an elaboration of the nature and structure of pre-predicative experience as it is portrayed by Husserl.

§ 23. Even the most primitive experience is *not* atomic. Discrete sense-data are not the absolute firsts that are given.[2] It is one of the fundamental errors of British empiricism that it

---

[1] *E.u.U.*, p. 3.
[2] *Krisis*, pp. 27–28 f; also, p. 96.

starts with what are rather possible data for subsequent abstractive attention.[1] Thus, at one stroke, Husserl goes beyond contemporary phenomenalism. He prefers, using more recent terminology, the language of physical object with its qualities to the sense-datum language.[2]

Coming to physical objects, again, there are two errors to be avoided. An isolated object is never given as such: it is always given as belonging to an environment, or more precisely, to a *field*.[3] In the next place, it would be wrong to think that an object (even within its *field*) is given as fully determinate. There is rather always something *to be determined*. In other words, no object is given all at once totally or adequately. By avoiding these two errors, Husserl also goes beyond the more usual forms of direct realism. These two aspects are combined in his notion of '*horizon*' [4] which, accordingly, splits up into two subordinate notions: that of the '*outer*' horizon and that of the '*inner*' horizon.

To take up the second of these first: every object of experience is not only capable of further determination, but points towards possibilities of such determination. This again happens in two ways: first, there is always the possibility of progressively *explicating* the content of what has already been given, and then there is the possibility of passing on to new features of the object. Now, with regard to the possibilities of new discoveries about the same object – there is a sort of *Vorwissen*, a pre-cognition which is not quite empty, for the general line of possible determination is certainly anticipated. It is in this sense, i.e., as comprehending both the given and the anticipated, that the physical object itself - and not merely its aspects – is given. For, *to be anticipated is also a mode of being intended* and hence also *a way of being given*. In the words of a recent writer,[5] the perceptual object "is apprehended incompletely but is not apprehended as incomplete"; the perception that something is a

---

[1] *E.u.U.*, p. 75.

[2] In *Krisis*, p. 28 f, he writes: "*Wir sprechen, hier und überall, getreu die wirkliche Erfahrung zur Aussprache bringend, von Qualitäten, von Eigenschaften der wirklich in diesen Eigenschaften wahrgenommenen Körper.*"

[3] *E.u.U.*, p. 24.

[4] *ibid.*, § 8.

[5] C. M. Meyers, "The Determinate and Determinable Modes of Appearing," *Mind*, 1958, pp. 32–49; p. 34. This paper develops an account of perceptual experience closely following Husserl.

determinate object is not the same as the perception of all its determinate aspects. Determinate and determinable aspects together constitute the given: the object is never given totally i.e. in all its possible determinations.

Coming from the 'inner' horizon to the 'outer,' we find that a given object also anticipates the other co-objects of the same *field*. Although at this moment I am not experiencing many of these objects, I might experience them: what is real can be experienced, so that it belongs to the indeterminate, but determinable horizon of my experienced actuality of any moment.[1]

Taking both horizons together into consideration, we may say that nothing is entirely unknown, for the unknown is known as unknown and in that sense to be unknown is already a mode of being known.[2] For we are acquainted with the unknown as belonging to *the world* which is the all-comprehensive horizon of all actual and possible experiences. Thus, there is a sense in which one could even say that *the world as a whole is always passively pregiven*, prior to all self-consciously directed activity of thought. For the *world* in this sense is not the static totality of all objects but the endless horizon – a system of intentionality and anticipation – within which the given leads to the not-yet given.

A truly phenomenological description of perceptual experience would thus avoid the errors connected with either a phenomenalistic or a physicalistic atomism.

The atomists, whether they are phenomenalists or physicalists, have to take recourse either to psychological principles (of habit and association) or to logical principles for constructing the world out of the elements. Phenomenology abandons the atomistic conception of the given in all its forms, and should therefore introduce the notions of associativity, habituality, inducibility, in short, the idea of *motivation* as necessary for describing the nature of *the given itself*.

Association in its most primitive form is the phenomenon that something points towards some other thing.[3] Association in this sense is nothing other than the horizontal character of experience. An allied phenomenon may be brought under the title

---

[1] *Ideen*, p. 112: "*es gehöre zum unbestimmten, aber bestimmbaren Horizont meiner jeweiligen Erfahrungsaktualität.*"

[2] "*... Unbekanntheit ist jederzeit zugleich ein Modus der Bekanntheit.*" (*E.u.U.*, p. 34).

[3] *E.u.U.*, p. 78.

'*interest*.' [1] Interest in the broad sense in which it characterizes experience is not the character of a specific act of volition: it is rather a feature which belongs to all perception. A perceptual experience gives rise to fresh expectations and is itself the fulfilment of a prior expectation. Concrete perception is permeated by such *a tendency* – or, rather by a manifold of tendencies – towards continuous self-expansion.[2] Interest and association serve the purpose of grouping together the like and separating them from the unlike, but all this takes place within the sphere of passive receptivity of experience. This again explains the fact that already our primitive experience is characterized by a certain vague *typicality* and is not a mere chaotic flow of evanescent states. Nothing occurs twice, it is true; but nevertheless a certain approximate typicality [3] is found operative from the very beginning as a result of – or, better as the correlate of – associativity and interest. In practical life, such a vague typicality [4] suffices for the purpose of identification: it is only at the level of reflective thought that this vague typicality is *transformed* into the precise universal with its ideal objectivity.[5]

There is another group of related phenomena which could be brought under the heading of '*Habituality*.' The things of the environment have their habits to behave similarly under similar circumstances. Even the world as a whole, Husserl tells us,[6] has its habituality, its "*empirischen Gestamtstil*" which it tends to retain (and which would be made thematic only in reflective thought). Husserl does not raise the problem of *justifying* this uniformity of nature, for uniformity in this broad sense of habituality [7] (which permits of being frustrated, thus making possible modal and negative judgments) is not a matter of theoretical belief but a phenomenological datum of our primitive experience of the environment. It is this more or less vague

---

[1] *ibid.*, § 20.

[2] "*So ist jede Wahrnehmungsphase ein Strahlensystem von aktuellen und potenziellen Erwartungsintentionen.*" (*E.u.U.*, p. 93).

[3] *Krisis*, p. 29.

[4] *Krisis*, p. 358.

[5] This transition from the vague typicality of pre-predicative experience to the ideal-objective universal of reflective thought is mediated by the 'presumptive universal' or the empirical class.

[6] *Krisis*, p. 28.

[7] This *Gesamtstil*, Husserl adds, is a "*leere Allgemeinheit*" and does not assume the definite laws of uniformity of the various sciences. (*Krisis*, p. 29).

habituality which makes inductive inference possible.[1] On induction in the sense of such foresight or general expectation all life rests. All practice is accompanied by such *Vorhaben*.[2] All perception has more than what is actual and contains a factor of *Vor-meinen*. There is thus a pre-predicative induction on which subsequent reflective scientific thought is based.

§ 24. It is only when experience is formulated in this manner that it becomes at least reasonably plausible to maintain that thought has its origin in experience. With an atomistic conception of experience, empiricism has the least chances of success in tracing thought back to an empirical origin: reductive analysis has therefore rightly come to be abandoned.

It may be granted that Husserl's conception of experience is far richer, far more true from a descriptive point of view, and has far greater explanatory power than the atomistic formulation; it still remains to be asked whether at all thought could be said to have its *origin* in such an experience.

Dewey's task in his *Experience and Nature* is largely similar to Husserl's in the *Krisis*, but is certainly much simpler, for Dewey never appreciated the ideal-objectivity of thought. He evinces a certain preparedness to grant objectivity to meanings, but, he adds,[3] that does not raise meanings above their basis in experience.

Husserl sees clearly the ideal-objectivity of meanings, but his empiricism leads him to search nevertheless for their origin in experience. This attempt to do justice to both aspects of the meaning-situation makes his task immensely difficult and his phenomenological empiricism a razor's edge to tread.

Husserl would largely agree with Dewey when the latter cautions us against the error of regarding common experience as incapable of developing from within itself methods "having inherent standards of judgment and value."[4]

Dewey also sees clearly, as much as Husserl does in the *Krisis*, the process by which Galileo converts the aesthetic object into

---

[1] *Krisis*, p. 29.
[2] *Krisis*, p. 51.
[3] Dewey, *Experience and Nature*, London, 1929, p. 195.
[4] *ibid.*, p. 38.

the scientific,[1] the world of qualities to the mathematical and the mechanical.[2]

Before Dewey, C. S. Peirce (a Platonic realist in his ontology) had tried to show – thereby anticipating Husserl more definitely – how concepts could have their origin in habits of belief which are, on their part, rooted in habits of action. Indeed, Peirce said that a habit was the biological embodiment of a general idea.[3] Following Peirce, Dewey held that universals were rooted in experience as plans or habits of decision, and came to formulate what he calls the 'principle of continuity' thus: "A general idea is simply a living and expanding feeling." [4]

The situation is indeed perplexing. In what sense, if at all, could we speak of the 'origin' of the ideal-objectivities of thought in experience, without doing violence to the phenomenological point of view? In other words, how can empiricism remain phenomenological without degenerating into reductionism? The suggestion made by Schuetz in a recent paper that "there is indeed merely a difference of degree between type and eidos," so that "Ideation can reveal nothing that was not preconstituted by the type," [5] does not seem to us to be acceptable. The principle of continuity, as Pringle Pattison pointed out in quite another context,[6] is *not* incompatible with the emergence of real differences. This is an important truth, and must be borne in mind in any phenomenological enquiry.

Husserl never lost his awareness of the fact that predicative thought was a new kind of 'objectifying act' whose creative spontaneity gave rise to a higher *Stockwerk*.[7] Nor did he fail to see that 'origination,' in the present context, has a totally different sense than when we speak of one real thing originating out of another.[8] It is highly plausible therefore to suggest that the vague typically characterizing original experience and the ideal-objective universal of thought do not differ merely in

[1] *ibid.*, p. 124.
[2] *ibid.*, p. 132.
[3] cp. H. Schneider, *A History of American Philosophy*, New York, 1946, p. 522.
[4] Quoted by Schneider, *ibid.*, p. 537.
[5] Alfred Schutz, "Type and Eidos in Husserl's Late Philosophy," *Philosophy and Phenomenological Research*, Dec. 1959, 147–165.
[6] *Idea of God*, p. 103.
[7] *E.u.U.*, p. 233.
[8] *ibid.*, p. 235.

degree: the latter originates in the former only in a highly metaphorical sense of 'origination.' One could as well simply say that the habitualities and typicalities are what *correspond within pre-predicative experience* to the universals of thought. *To say more than that would be going beyond phenomenology* and taking recourse either to a reductive analysis or to a deductive metaphysics.

That 'origination' is to be understood here only in a metaphorical sense is also clear from Husserl's strenuous attempts to describe the process of idealisation, for this process is found to involve the inevitable *immer wieder*, an endless process of reiteration.[1] Without going into the details of his account, it might still be said that a method that involves an endless process could *not* be actually completed so as to result in the real production of the idealities. All descriptions of this process are therefore to be understood as attempts of reflective thought to bridge the gulf between experience and thought, but they teach the lesson that the gulf cannot be bridged, that a *certain phenomenological discontinuity* [2] has to be recognized as being ultimate.

---

[1] cp. *Beilage* II (aus 1936(?)) to *Krisis*, especially pp. 359 ff. An account of this process is also to be found in *Krisis*, pp. 370 ff.

[2] cp. J. N. Mohanty, "Individual Fact and Essence in Edmund Husserl's Philosophy," *Philosophy and Phenomenological Research*, Dec. 1959, pp. 222–230.

BIBLIOGRAPHICAL REFERENCES

The primary sources used in this book are those works of Husserl which have been mentioned in the note on Abbreviations given at the beginning of the book. The list given below includes only the names of such works as have been alluded to in the course of the book.

BOOKS

Ayer, A. J., *Thinking and Meaning*, London, 1947.

Anscombe, G. E. M., *Intention*, Oxford, 1957.

Bergmann, G., *Metaphysics of Logical Positivism*, Longmans Green, 1954.

Black, M., *Problems of Analysis*, Cornell, 1954.

Blanshard, B., *The Nature of Thought*, 2 Vols., London, 1939.

Buber, M., *Urdistanz und Beziehung*, Heidelberg, 1951.

Buchler (ed), *Philosophical Writings of C. S. Peirce*, New York, 1955.

Bühler, K., *Sprachtheorie*, 1934.

Carnap, R., *Logical Syntax of Language*, London and New York, 1937.

Carnap, R., *Introduction to Semantics*, Cambridge, Mass., 1942.

Croce, B., *Aesthetics*, London, 1909.

Dewey, J., *Experience and Nature*, London, 1929.

Flew, A., *Logic and Language*. Second Series. Oxford, 1955.

Goodman, N., *The Structure of Appearance*, Harvard, 1951.

Heidegger, M., *Einführung in die Metaphysik*, Tübingen, 1953.

— *Über den Humanismus*, Bern, 1954.

— *Was heisst Denken?*, Tübingen, 1954.

—, *Vorträge und Aufsätze*, Pfullingen, 1954.

Heveni, J. L. (ed), *Essays on Language and Literature*, London.

Humboldt, W. v., *Über die Verschiedenheit des menschlichen Sprachbaues*, Darmstadt edn., 1949.

Linsky (ed) –, *Semantics and the Philosophy of Language*, Illinois, 1952.

Lipps, H., *Untersuchungen zu einer hermeneutischen Logik*, Frankfurt, 1938.

Mill, J. S., *An Examination of Sir W. Hamilton's Philosophy*, 3rd. ed., London, 1867.

Price, H. H., *Thinking and Experience*, London, 1953.

Quine, W. V. O., *Methods of Logic*, Routledge & Kegan Paul, 1951.

—, *From a Logical Point of View*, Harvard, 1953.

Parain, B., *Recherches sur la nature et les fonctions du langage*, Paris, 1942.

Russell, B., *Introduction to Mathematical Philosophy*, London, 1919.

—, *Inquiry into Meaning and Truth*, London, 1940.

—, *Human Knowledge, Its Scope and Limits*, London, 1948.

—, *Logic and Knowledge*, London, 1956.

Schneider, H., *A History of American Philosophy*, New York, 1946.
Stebbing, L. S., *A Modern Introduction to Logic*, London, 5th. ed., 1946.
Stout, G. F., *Studies in Philosophy and Psychology*, London, 1930.
Tarski, A., *Introduction to Logic*, New York, 1941.
Van Breda, H. L. (ed), *Problèms actuels de la phénoménologie*, Bruxelles, 1952.
Veatch, *Intentional Logic*, Yale, 1952.
Warnock, G. J., *Berkeley*, 1953.
—, *English Philosophy since 1900*, Oxford, 1958.
Weyl, H., *Philosophy of Mathematics and Natural Science*, Princeton, 1949.
White, M., *Reunion in Philosophy*, Harvard, 1956.
Whorf, B. L., *Language, Thought and Reality*, edited by J. B. Carrol, 1956.
Wittgenstein, L., *Philosophical Investigations*, Oxford, 1953.

ARTICLES

Bar-Hillel, Y., "Husserl's Conception of a purely Logical Grammar," *Philosophy and Phenomenological Research*, 1956.
Chisholm, R., "Review of Anscombe's Intention," *The Philosophical Review*, 1959.
Evans, J. L., "On Meaning and Verification," *Mind*, 1953.
Frege, G., "Über Sinn und Bedeutung" *Zeitschrift für Philosophie und philosophische Kritik*, N.F. 100, 1892.
Geach, P. T., "Subject and Predicate," *Mind*, 1950.
Goodman, N., "On Likeness of Meaning" (in Linsky, cf. above).
Lenneberg, "A Note on Cassirer's Philosophy of Language," *Philosophy and Phenomenological Research*, 1954.
Lewis, C. I., "The Modes of Meaning" (in *Linsky*).
Meyers, C. M., "The Determinate and Determinable Modes of Appearing," *Mind*, 1958.
Mohanty, J. N., "Types of Linguistic Philosophy," *The Viswabharati Quarterly*, Vol. 25, No. 2.
—, "Individual Fact and Essence in Edmund Husserl's Philosophy," *Philosophy and Phenomenological Research*, 1959.
Popper, K., "Language and the Body-Mind Problem," *Proceedings of the XIth. International Congress of Philosophy*, Vol. VII.
Pos, H. J., "Phenoménologie et linguistique," *Revue Internationale de Philosophie*, 1939.
Quine, W. V. O., "Designation and Existence," *Journal of Philosophy*, 1939.
—, "Semantics and Abstract Objects," *Proceedings of the American Academy of Arts and Sciences*, Vol. 80, no. 1.
—, "Two Dogmas of Empiricism," *The Philosophical Review*, 1951.
—, "Mr. Strawson on Logical Theory," *Mind*, 1953.
Ryle, G., "Systematically Misleading Expressions," *Proceedings of the Aristotelian Society*, 1931–32.
—, "Meaning and Necessity," *Philosophy*, 1949.
—, "Theory of Meaning" (in Mace(ed), *British Philosophy in Mid-century*).
Schuetz, A., "Type and Eidos in Husserl's Late Philosophy," *Philosophy and Phenomenological Research*, 1959.

Strawson, P. F., "On Referring," *Mind*, 1950.
—, "Singular Terms, Ontology and Identity," *Mind*, 1956.
Taylor, R., "Disputes about Synonymy," *The Philosophical Review*, 1954.
White, M., "The Analytic and the Synthetic" (in *Linsky*).
Whorf, B. L., "Language, Mind and Reality," *Theosophist*, 1942.

INDEX OF PROPER NAMES